Survey Research Methods

4 EDITION

APPLIED SOCIAL RESEARCH METHODS SERIES

Series Editors
LEONARD BICKMAN, Peabody College, Vanderbilt University, Nashville
DEBRA J. ROG, Westat

Survey
Research
Methods

4 EDITION

Floyd J. Fowler, Jr.

Center for Survey Research
University of Massachusetts Boston

1 APPLIED SOCIAL RESEARCH METHODS SERIES
Edited by Leonard Bickman and Debra J. Rog

Los Angeles • London • New Delhi • Singapore • Washington DC

Copyright © 2009 by SAGE Publications, Inc.

All rights reserved. No part of this book may be reproduced or utilized in any form or by any means, electronic or mechanical, including photocopying, recording, or by any information storage and retrieval system, without permission in writing from the publisher.

For information:

SAGE Publications, Inc.
2455 Teller Road
Thousand Oaks, California 91320
E-mail: order@sagepub.com

SAGE Publications Ltd.
1 Oliver's Yard
55 City Road
London EC1Y 1SP
United Kingdom

SAGE Publications India Pvt. Ltd.
B 1/I 1 Mohan Cooperative
  Industrial Area
Mathura Road, New Delhi 110 044
India

SAGE Publications Asia-Pacific
  Pte. Ltd.
33 Pekin Street #02-01
Far East Square
Singapore 048763

Printed in the United States of America

Library of Congress Cataloging-in-Publication Data

Fowler, Floyd J. Survey research methods / Floyd J Fowler, Jr.—4th ed.
    p. cm.—(Applied social research methods series)
Includes bibliographical references and index.
ISBN 978-1-4129-5841-7 (pbk.)
  1. Social surveys. I. Title.

HN29.F68 2009
300.72'3—dc22   2008011835

This book is printed on acid-free paper.

          10   11   12   10   9   8   7   6   5   4   3

Acquisitions Editor:	Vicki Knight
Editorial Assistant:	Lauren Habib
Production Editor:	Astrid Virding
Typesetter:	C&M Digitals (P) Ltd
Proofreader:	Dennis W. Webb
Indexer:	Jeanne R. Busemeyer
Cover Designer:	Candice Harman
Marketing Manager:	Stephanie Adams

Contents

Preface

The goal of this fourth edition of *Survey Research Methods,* like its predecessors, is to produce a summary of the basic concepts and current knowledge about sources of error in surveys for those who are not primarily statisticians or methodologists. Surveys are fundamentally a matter of asking a sample of people from a population a set of questions and using the answers to describe that population. How the sample is selected, which questions are asked, and the procedures used to collect the answers all have the potential to affect how well the survey is likely to accomplish its goals. If one is going to commission a survey or use survey data collected by others, it is important to understand why these issues matter and how they affect survey results. Readers should have that understanding by the time they finish this book.

Considerable effort has been made to make this book accessible to a general audience. Although familiarity with social science research and statistical concepts is a plus, no special background should be required to grasp the material in this book.

This is also designed to be a comparatively brief book. Choices have been made about the level of depth given to the various topics. Throughout the book, there are suggestions for further reading for those whose interests go beyond an introductory level.

NEW IN THE FOURTH EDITION

This edition contains two new chapters that were not in previous editions. Error in surveys is potentially confusing because there at least four different kinds of potential error that survey methodology is designed to minimize. When I have taught survey methods, I often have devoted a class solely to the topic of the nature of error in surveys. In previous editions, those concepts were distributed throughout the book as they seemed relevant. A new Chapter 2, "Types of Error in Surveys," now introduces those concepts up front.

In a similar way, the implications of the sample design and nonresponse for the analysis of survey data were discussed as they became relevant throughout earlier editions. Since these issues usually are addressed after data have been collected, a new Chapter 10, "Analyzing Survey Data," concentrates the discussion of how to address these issues during analysis after all of the data collection topics have been covered.

In the 6 years since the third edition was published, one of the biggest emerging issues in survey methodology is increased concern about the future of telephone surveys as the main way to collect data about the general population. At the same time, there is a major effort to try to figure out how to use the Internet most effectively. Both of these developments are works in progress as this edition is completed, but this edition reflects an effort to put both in perspective, even as we know that practices will continue to evolve. In addition, of course, this edition integrates new studies and publications from the past 6 years.

ACKNOWLEDGMENTS

Finally, doing justice to the people who have contributed to making this book what it is gets harder, as the list inevitably grows with each edition. I think it is still appropriate to start with the three people who probably had the most effect on my understanding of survey research methods: Robert Kahn, Morris Axelrod, and Charles Cannell. In many respects, the task of the book is to pull together and summarize what others have written and learned, so the references and, in particular, those suggested for further reading were key resources. However, the name of Robert Groves is probably found as often as any other in this edition, and that certainly reflects his large and varied contributions to the field of survey research.

I would also like to specifically thank Tony Roman, Mary Ellen Colten, Trish Gallagher, and Dragana Bolcic-Jankovic for their reviews and helpful comments on various chapters. We would like to thank the reviewers, Mark Berends, Vanderbilt University; Adam Berinsky, Massachusetts Institute of Technology; Amie L. Nielsen, University of Miami; and Patric R. Spence, Western Kentucky University, who provided feedback on the 3rd edition that helped to shape the 4th edition. The Center for Survey Research provided critical support services. Judy Chambliss, as always, played a crucial role in helping me to maintain the mental health this effort required. I thank these and others for their contributions, but the responsibility for the final product, good and bad, is basically mine.

Jack Fowler

1

Introduction

This book is about standards and practical procedures for surveys designed to provide statistical descriptions of people by asking questions, usually of a sample. Surveys meld sampling, question design, and data collection methodologies. Those who want to collect, analyze, or read about survey data will learn how details of each aspect of a survey can affect its precision, accuracy, and credibility.

The subject of this book is data collection in social surveys. It includes common procedures, standards for good practice, and the implications of various design decisions for the quality of survey data. The purpose of the book is to give a sound basis for evaluating data collection procedures to those who would collect, analyze, or read about survey data. Readers will come to understand the ways in which the details of data collection are related to the confidence they can have in figures and statistics based on surveys.

There are many data collection and measurement processes that are called surveys. This book focuses on those surveys that have the following characteristics:

- The purpose of the survey is to produce statistics, that is, quantitative or numerical descriptions about some aspects of the study population.

- The main way of collecting information is by asking people questions; their answers constitute the data to be analyzed.

- Generally, information is collected about only a fraction of the population, that is, a sample, rather than from every member of the population.

REASONS FOR SURVEYS

In the U.S. Constitution, it is specified that a survey meeting the above criteria must be carried out every 10 years. In the decennial census, statistics are produced about a population by asking people questions. No sampling, though, is involved; data are supposed to be collected about every person in the population.

The purpose of the decennial census is to count people as a basis for ensuring appropriate representation in the House of Representatives. The census,

1

however, also has become a major source of information for many other purposes. In addition to simple counts, it collects data about the race, age, household composition, education, type of housing, and many other characteristics of the people counted.

The content of the decennial census has expanded to meet the needs of government agencies and researchers for descriptive data. It covers only a small portion of what people want to know about populations, however, and its value is limited because it occurs only once per decade. To provide data to fill those information gaps, special-purpose surveys have become a prevalent part of American life since the 1930s.

Most people are familiar with three uses of survey techniques: the measurement of public opinion for newspaper and magazine articles, the measurement of political perceptions and opinions to help political candidates in elections, and market research designed to understand consumer preferences and interests. Each of these well-developed programs of survey research is aimed primarily at tapping the subjective feelings of the public. There are, in addition, numerous facts about the behaviors and situations of people that can be obtained only by asking a sample of people about themselves. There probably is no area of public policy to which survey research methodology has not been applied. The following is an abbreviated list of some of the major applications:

• Unemployment rates, as released routinely by the Bureau of Labor Statistics, as well as many other statistics about jobs and work, are based on household surveys carried out by the Bureau of the Census. Parallel surveys of businesses and industries are carried out to describe production and manpower needs.

• People's incomes and the way they spend their money constitute another area in which only surveys can provide reliable data. Patterns of consumer expenditures and their expectations have proven to be important predictors of trends in the economy.

• The National Health Interview Survey has been carried out by the Bureau of the Census for the National Center for Health Statistics since the late 1950s. This survey collects basic data about health conditions, use of health services, and behaviors that affect the risk of illness. These are all topics about which only good survey research can provide adequate data.

• The main source of data about criminal events traditionally has been police department records. Police records, however, only include events that people report to the police. For most crimes involving victims, surveys provide more reliable measures of the rates at which crimes occur and the characteristics of the victims. The National Crime Survey was launched in the 1970s to provide such figures. In addition, surveys are the only way to measure people's concerns and fears about crime.

- One of the oldest applications of surveys is by the U.S. Department of Agriculture. The department surveys farmers to estimate the rate at which different crops will be planted and to predict the availability of various food products.

- Mental health, transportation needs and patterns of use, political behavior, characteristics of housing such as its cost and appropriateness to familial needs, and worker satisfaction are other examples of areas where survey research is used extensively. The largest collector of survey data in the United States is undoubtedly the federal government, particularly the Bureau of the Census and the Department of Agriculture. In addition, thousands of individual surveys are done each year by university, nonprofit, and for-profit survey organizations.

Sponsoring a special-purpose survey data collection is a rather expensive solution to an information problem. Before launching such an effort, one should explore thoroughly the potential for gathering the same information from existing records or from other sources. Although some people think of a survey as a first effort to try to learn something about a population, a full-scale probability sample survey should be undertaken only after it is certain that the information cannot be obtained in other ways. Even taking such a conservative approach, it is common to find that only a special-purpose survey can provide the information that is needed. In addition to meeting needs for data that are not available elsewhere, there are three potential properties of data from a properly done survey that may make them preferable to data from other sources:

- *Probability sampling* enables one to have confidence that the sample is not a biased one and to estimate how precise the data are likely to be. Data from a properly chosen sample are a great improvement over data from a sample of those who attend meetings, speak loudest, write letters, or happen to be convenient to poll.

- *Standardized measurement* that is consistent across all respondents ensures that comparable information is obtained about everyone who is described. Without such measurement, meaningful statistics cannot be produced.

- To meet analysis needs, a *special-purpose survey* may be the only way to ensure that all the data needed for a given analysis are available and can be related. Even if there is information about some set of events, it may not be paired with other characteristics needed to carry out a desired analysis. For example, hospital discharge records invariably lack information about income. Hence a survey that collects both income and hospitalization data about people is needed in order to study the relationship between a person's income and hospitalization experience.

There is always some information available on a given topic from what people say, from impressions, or from records; there also are always imperfections in available data. In addition to an assessment of information needs, the decision to do a survey also should depend on available staff resources. Unless the needed staff and expertise, or the resources to buy them, are available, the data resulting from a survey may not be very good. That brings us to the topic of the next section: What constitutes a good survey?

COMPONENTS OF SURVEYS

Like all measures in all sciences, social survey measurement is not error free. The procedures used to conduct a survey have a major effect on the likelihood that the resulting data will describe accurately what they are intended to describe.

A sample survey brings together three different methodologies: sampling, designing questions, and data collection. Each of these activities has many applications outside of sample surveys, but their combination is essential to good survey design.

Sampling

A *census* means gathering information about every individual in a population. A major development in the process of making surveys useful was learning how to *sample:* to select a small subset of a population representative of the whole population. The keys to good sampling are finding a way to give all (or nearly all) population members the same (or a known) chance of being selected and using probability methods for choosing the sample. Early surveys and polls often relied on samples of convenience or on sampling from lists that excluded significant portions of the population. These did not provide reliable, credible figures.

The Department of Agriculture actually developed the procedures for drawing the comprehensive probability samples needed to provide statistically reliable descriptions of populations living in a definable area. The procedures evolved from work designed to sample land areas for predicting crop yields; sampling housing units and the people living in those housing units was simply an extension of that work. During World War II, a group of social scientists was housed in the Department of Agriculture to do social surveys related to the war effort. It was then that area probability sampling became firmly entrenched for sampling general populations in social surveys. Area probability sampling is still the method of choice for personal interview surveys of households. Converse (1987) provides an excellent description of the evolution of survey methods in the United States.

Strategies for sampling have been refined since 1950. One major advance was the development of random-digit dialing (RDD), which permitted the inclusion of households in telephone surveys that did not have listed telephone numbers (Waksberg, 1978). The principles of good sampling practice, however, have been well developed for a long time.

Question Design

Using questions as measures is another essential part of the survey process. The initial survey efforts, representing extensions of journalism, were not careful about the way that questions were posed. It soon became apparent, however, that sending an interviewer out with a set of question objectives without providing specific wording for the questions produced important differences in the answers that were obtained. Thus, early in the 20th century, researchers began to write standardized questions for measuring subjective phenomena. Again, researchers at the U.S. Department of Agriculture are given credit for extending the use of standardized questions in the 1940s to situations in which factual or objective information was sought. Payne (1951) published a landmark book providing practical guidelines for writing clear questions that interviewers could administer as worded. Likert (1932) generally is credited for building a bridge between the elaborate scaling techniques developed by psychophysical psychologists for measuring subjective phenomena (e.g., Thurstone & Chave, 1929) and the practical requirements of applied social survey research.

The major advance in question design in the last 20 years has been improved strategies for evaluating questions. More than before, researchers now evaluate questions to find out if they are well understood and if the answers are meaningful (see Presser et al., 2004). Pretests of surveys have become more systematic, using analyses of tape-recorded interviews to identify problem questions. As a result, the choice of question wording is becoming more objective and less a matter of research judgment.

Interviewing

Although not all surveys involve interviewing (as some surveys have respondents answer self-administered questions), it certainly is common to use an interviewer to ask questions and record answers. When interviewers are used, it is important to avoid having them influence the answers respondents give, and at the same time to maximize the accuracy with which questions are answered. The first major step in increasing interviewer consistency was to give them standardized questions. It subsequently was found that interviewers also needed to be trained in how to administer a survey so as to avoid introducing important biases in the answers they obtained (Friedman, 1942). Hyman, Feldman, and Stember (1954) published a series of studies documenting ways other than question wording that interviewers could influence the answers they obtained. Their work led to more elaborate training of interviewers with respect to strategies for probing when incomplete answers are obtained and for handling the interpersonal aspects of the interview in nonbiasing ways. Cannell, Oksenberg, and Converse (1977) advanced the process of trying to reduce between-interviewer variation by specifically scripting the introductions and encouragement that interviewers provide to respondents, while limiting unstructured discussion. The importance of interviewer training and supervision for ensuring data quality has now been well documented (Billiet & Loosveldt, 1988; Fowler & Mangione, 1990).

Mode of Data Collection

Until the 1970s, most academic and government surveys were done by in-person, household interviewers. When telephone ownership became nearly universal in the United States, telephone interviewing became a major mode of data collection. The current frontier for data collection is the Internet. At the moment, its use is limited because many people lack Internet access and because the lists and strategies for sampling e-mail addresses are limited. However, as access increases and sampling strategies evolve, the use of the Internet to collect survey data will certainly increase as well.

Total Survey Design

In many ways, the principles for good research practice were well developed in the 1950s. However, understandably, the procedures and tools have changed in response to new technologies and scientific advances. In some cases, we lack good studies of how best to collect data for a particular purpose. However, even when best practices have been well established, there is variability in the quality of the procedures that are used.

There are many reasons for variation in the quality of surveys. For some surveys, imprecise figures will suffice. Lack of funding and of adequate staff, as well as lack of methodological knowledge, no doubt all contribute to poor practice in some cases. There also are some controversies about the value of strict probability sampling and standardized question wording (see Converse, 1987; Groves, 1989; Schober & Conrad, 1997; Turner & Martin, 1984). One feature of survey research design that is partly to blame, however, is the failure of researchers to put together high-quality procedures in all three of the salient areas; it is not uncommon to see researchers attend carefully to some aspects of good survey design at the same time as they neglect others. A critical orientation of this book is the so-called total survey design perspective.

Every survey involves a number of decisions that have the potential to enhance or detract from the accuracy (or precision) of survey estimates. Generally, the decisions that would lead one to have better data involve more money, time, or other resources. Thus the design of a survey involves a set of decisions to optimize the use of resources. Optimal design will take into account all the salient aspects of the survey process.

With respect to sampling, critical issues include the following:

- the choice of whether or not to use a probability sample
- the sample frame (those people who actually have a chance to be sampled)
- the size of the sample
- the sample design (the particular strategy used for sampling people or households)
- the rate of response (the percentage of those sampled for whom data are actually collected)

With respect to question design, the researcher must decide the extent to which previous literature regarding the reliability and validity of questions will be drawn upon, the use to be made of consultants who are experts in question design, and the investment to be made in pre-testing and question evaluation. With respect to interviewers, researchers have choices to make about the amount and kind of training and supervision to give. A design decision cutting across all these areas is the mode of data collection: whether the researcher will collect data by telephone, by mail, by personal interview, over the Internet, or in some other way and how, if at all, computers will be involved. The decision about which mode of data collection to use has important cost implications and affects the quality of the data that will be collected.

These pieces, taken together, constitute what is called the *total survey design*. The components of the design are interrelated in two important ways. First, the quality of data will be no better than the most error-prone feature of the survey design. In the past, researchers sometimes have focused on one or two features of the survey, such as the size of the sample or the response rate, to evaluate the likely quality of data. Current best practice, however, requires examination of all of the above design features. If there is a major compromise or weakness in any aspect of the survey design, major investments in other portions of the survey are not sensible. For example, if one is asking questions that respondents are unlikely to be able to answer with great precision, a very large sample aimed at reducing sampling error to a minimum is likely to be unwarranted. Similarly, and perhaps even more common, a large number of survey responses will not increase credibility if the sample is poorly designed, if the rate of response is so low as to make the sample unlikely to be representative, or if the interviewers are poorly trained and supervised.

For designers and users of survey research, the total survey design approach means asking questions about all of these features, not just a few, when attempting to evaluate the quality of a survey and the credibility of a particular data set.

PURPOSES AND GOALS OF THIS TEXT

This text presents a discussion of the major decisions that go into the design of any survey research project, the options available to the researcher, and the potential significance of the various options for the amount of error and the credibility of survey estimates. When appropriate, a set of procedures that would constitute good survey practice is presented. A serious effort is made to discuss the realities and the practical problems with which researchers must wrestle, as well as the theoretical and methodological issues at stake; many of the shortcomings of data collections stem from faulty execution of details rather than a lack of general understanding.

A book of this relatively short length obviously has to reflect a set of choices. Entire books can be, and have been, devoted to topics such as sampling, questionnaire design, and research on interviewers. Persons planning to carry out survey research projects will want to read further. Moreover, reading a book such as this (or any book) is no substitute for practical apprenticeship and training with experts who have both sound methodological backgrounds and extensive experience in the design and execution of surveys. Nevertheless, there is an important role that this book, by itself, can play: to provide a comprehensive overview of the sources of error and the range of methodological issues in survey data collection.

There are many people for whom such understanding will be appropriate and valuable. Certainly social scientists who use data collected by others in their work should have a sophisticated understanding of the sources of error.

In the same way, people who read about statistics based on surveys need to understand the data collection process. This book identifies the questions that people who use data need to ask and to have answered. In addition, it provides the overview that those who are considering purchasing or commissioning a survey need to have. In short, this book is intended to provide perspective and understanding to those who would be designers or users of survey research, at the same time that it provides a sound first step for those who actually may go about collecting data.

2

Types of Error in Surveys

Surveys are designed to produce statistics about a target population. The process by which this is done rests on inferring the characteristics of the target population from the answers provided by a sample of respondents. This chapter outlines the two kinds of inferences that are required. It also describes the two types of error, bias and variability, that can limit the accuracy of those inferences.

Two of the main goals of survey methodology are to minimize error in data collected by surveys and to measure the error that necessarily is part of any survey. Chapters 3 through 9 describe in detail strategies for minimizing and measuring error. In order to appreciate those chapters, and to understand survey methodology, it is first necessary to understand what we mean by *error.*

As we have said, the purpose of a survey is to provide statistical estimates of the characteristics of a target population, some set of people. To do that we designate a subset of that population, a sample, from whom we try to collect information. *One fundamental premise of the survey process is that by describing the sample of people who actually respond, one can describe the target population.* The hope is that the characteristics the survey is designed to describe are present to the same degree, and are distributed in the same way, in the sample responding as in the target population as a whole.

The other defining characteristic of a survey is that respondents answer questions. The answers to the questions are used to describe the experiences, opinions, and other characteristics of those answering the questions. *A second fundamental premise of the survey research process is that the answers people give can be used to accurately describe characteristics of the respondents.* The extent to which those answers are not accurate measures is the second fundamental source of error in surveys.

Figure 2.1 shows in graphic form the way analysis of survey data works and the inferences on which it is based. The goal is to learn the characteristics of the target population. The material we have to work with consists of the answers the respondents gave in the survey. We tabulate the answers and would like to make the assumption that the answers are accurate measures of the characteristics of the respondents we are trying to measure. We then would

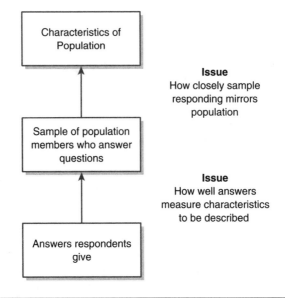

Figure 2.1   Inference in Survey Research

like to be able to further assume that by describing the sample of respondents, we are accurately describing the entire target population.

Some aspects of survey methodology are designed to address how closely a sample of respondents mirrors the population. Some aspects of survey methodology are designed to address how well the answers to the questions collected in the survey serve as measures of what they are intended to measure. The design of the survey and the way data collection is carried out can affect one or both of these potential sources of error.

ERROR ASSOCIATED WITH WHO ANSWERS

Any time a sample is drawn from a larger population, there is some chance that by chance alone that sample will differ from the total population from which it was drawn. A simple example that statisticians like to use is flipping a coin, which is heads on one side and tails on the other. Even if the coin is perfectly fair, a sample of 10 flips will not always produce 5 heads and 5 tails. While 5 heads and 5 tails will be most common, a certain number of samples of 10 flips will produce 6 heads or 4 heads; 3 and 7 heads will be less common; 8 or 2 heads will be even less common; even more extreme distributions will be increasingly less common, but even those will occur if enough samples of 10 flips of a coin are actually tried. In the same way, if a population consists of 50% males and 50% females, any particular sample may by chance have more or fewer females than one would expect from the population as a whole.

In a sample survey, we usually only have a single sample from which to generalize. By chance, that sample can and will differ slightly from what it would look like if it perfectly mirrored the distribution of characteristics in the population. One goal of survey methodology is to minimize the random differences between the sample and the population. The way the sample is designed and selected can affect how closely the sample is likely to mirror the characteristics of the population from which it is drawn.

One kind of error of concern to survey methodologists is this random variation from the true characteristics of the population. This variation, the possible error that stems solely from the fact that data are collected from a sample rather than from every single member of the population, is called *sampling error*. It is one kind of error survey methodologists try to minimize.

A second kind of error that affects the relationship between a sample of respondents and of the population is *bias*. Bias means that in some systematic way the people responding to a survey are different from the target population as a whole.

There are three steps in the process of collecting data from a sample, each of which could, potentially, introduce bias into a sample:

1. The first step involves choosing the *sample frame,* those who actually have a chance to be selected. If there are some people in the target population who do not have any chance at all to be selected for the sample, and if they are somehow consistently different from those who do have a chance to be selected, the resulting sample will be biased in those ways. As an example, most surveys in the United States leave out people who live in group homes, such as prisons, convents, and nursing homes, and they leave out people who have no home address at all. Most telephone surveys not only leave out those without any telephone service at all but also those households that only have cell phones. For variables on which those people who are included are different from those who are systematically left out, the samples from whom data are collected will be biased as well.

2. If somehow the *process of selecting* who is in the sample is not random, the result could be a sample of respondents who are different from the target population as a whole. For example, if a sample consists of people who volunteer to be in a survey, they are likely to have a different profile of interests than those who do not volunteer.

3. Finally, *failure to collect answers from everyone* selected to be in the sample is a third potential source of bias. Some people are not available to answer questions; some people are unable to answer questions, due to their health or their language skills; some people refuse to answer the questions. To the extent that those who are unavailable, unable, or unwilling to answer questions are different from the rest of the population in ways that affect the survey answers, the results of the survey may be biased.

It is important to understand the distinction between the two kinds of errors in data. Sampling error, the first kind of error that was discussed, is random error. By chance, sometimes there will be too many females in the sample, sometimes too few, but on average, a series of properly drawn samples will have very close to the same percentage of females as the population as a whole. A challenge for methodologists is to minimize the variability from sample to sample to increase the likelihood that any given sample is very close to the population as a whole.

In contrast, features of the design or execution of a survey that bias samples will, on average, produce estimates that are consistently different from the target population as whole. So, when samples are drawn only from those who live in households, excluding those who are homeless and live in group quarters, the average income is likely to be higher in those who respond than among those who had no chance to respond. Those in households also are more likely to be married and to have jobs than those without homes. Estimates from those responding to surveys based on households will systematically overestimate the percentage of the whole population that have those characteristics.

One final point to note is that the random variability of sample estimates, the sampling error, and the bias associated with a sample, are not necessarily related at all. If a survey plan systematically leaves out, or underrepresents, some people who are distinctive in ways relevant to the survey's goals, it is quite possible to have a very consistent and stable estimate, with very little sampling error, that is consistently biased and under- or overestimates some characteristics of the population.

ERROR ASSOCIATED WITH ANSWERS

In order to understand error associated with answers to survey questions, one first needs to understand what is being measured. In theory, one could divide what surveys try to measure into two categories: objective facts and subjective states. Objective facts include a person's height, whether or not a person is employed at a job, and whether or not a person voted in the last election. Subjective states include how much of the time the person has felt tired and whether or not a person has liberal or conservative political views.

Conceptually, the way we assess the answers to a question is to measure how well they correspond to the truth. If we are asking survey respondents about objective facts, such as their height or whether or not they are employed at a job, in theory we could obtain independent information against which to evaluate the answers to the survey question. We could measure the respondent's height; we could verify employment status by looking at records. We could directly assess how accurate the answers were. In contrast, there is no objective way to verify or evaluate a person's report about how much of the time he or she has felt tired.

Psychometricians, those who specialize in the measurement of psychological states, think of answers as consisting of two components: the true score, what a perfect reporter with perfect knowledge would give as an answer, plus some element of error.

$$x_i = t_i + e_i$$

Where

x_i is the answer given by individual i

t_i is the true value for individual i

e_i is the error in the answer given by individual i

Errors can be caused by all kinds of things: misunderstanding the question, not having the information needed to answer, and distorting answers in order to look good are only a few examples. Some respondents might not know their height exactly; others might round their height up or down, thinking that being taller or shorter might be more attractive. Respondents' estimates of how tired they have been over the past week may be affected by how tired they feel at the time they are answering the questions. The point is that to the extent that answers are affected by factors other than the facts on which the answer should be based, there is error in the answer.

Validity is the term that psychologists use to describe the relationship between an answer and some measure of the true score. Looking at the equation above, the goal of the psychometrician and the survey methodologist is to make the error term (e) as small as possible so the answers mainly reflect the true score (or answer).

In a way, the error term in psychometrics is similar to sampling error discussed previously. If the error associated with answers is random, resulting in answers that err sometimes in one direction, sometimes in another direction, the result is less certainty or confidence in how well the answers are measuring what we want to measure. The larger the value of e (in the equation above), the greater the chance that any individual's answer will be in error. However, across many answers from among individuals, the average answer should be the same as the average true value.

For questions designed to measure objective facts, but not subjective states, there also is the potential that answers will be biased. In a way completely analogous to bias with respect to the samples, what bias means in this context is that on average the errors in answers, the way in which answers differ from the true score, are more likely to be in one direction than another. As examples, respondents on average underreport how many cigarettes they smoke and how much alcohol they drink, while they tend to overstate whether or not they voted. Estimates of these behaviors are likely to be biased—systematically different from the true scores.

The idea of validity for subjective measures cannot be observed directly, but is inferred from studies of how answers are related to other similar measures. The calculations are more complicated, but the end results of estimates of validity are the same: an estimate of how well answers reflect the construct they are designed to measure. (Cronbach & Meehl, 1955; Saris & Andrews, 1991). In contrast, since we cannot directly measure the true value of subjective states, we also cannot measure bias—the degree to which answers systematically differ from a true score in one direction.

RECAPPING THE NATURE OF ERROR IN SURVEYS

Thus, for both of the key inferences that are critical to the quality of survey estimates, the inference that answers can be used to accurately describe a sample of respondents and that we can accurately generalize from a sample of respondents to an entire population, there are two analogous kinds of error: random variability around the true values and systematic (biased) differences between the samples who answer questions and the whole population or between the answers that are given and the true values for those who are answering. Throughout the book, as error is being discussed, readers need to be sure they know which kind of error is meant. Is it the problem of generalization from the sample of respondents to the population or generalization from the answers to the reality we want to describe? Is the concern with respect to error focused on minimizing random variation, variation that may by chance make our samples or our answers different from the true values of

TABLE 2.1
Examples of Error by Types of Error and Type of Inference

	Types of Error	
Inference	Random	Biased
From sample to population	Sampling error	Example: Those who are over 65 are consistently less likely to respond to telephone surveys, and hence are underrepresented in telephone survey data
From answers to true characteristics	Invalidity	Example: Number of cigarettes smoked is consistently underreported in surveys

the population, or is there some kind of systematic (biasing) error in our data, stemming either from having some elements of the population underrepresented in our sample of respondents or from some systematic distortion of answers to the questions that we posed? Table 2.1 graphically displays four kinds of error that affect our survey estimates.

When trying to evaluate the confidence one can have in estimates based on surveys, it is important to keep in mind all four of these kinds of error. They are different, they usually result from different aspects of the way a survey is executed, and they have different impacts on the ability of a survey to address the questions it is designed to answer.

Given this orientation to the various meanings of *error*, we now proceed to discuss the significance of the way a survey is designed and executed for the confidence one can have in the survey results.

Further Readings

Groves, R. M. (1989). *Survey errors and survey costs*. New York: John Wiley.
Groves, R. M., Fowler, F. J., Couper, M. P., Lepkowski, J. M., Singer, E., & Tourangeau, R. (2004). *Survey methodology* (Chap. 2). New York: John Wiley.
Lessler, J. T., & Kalsbeek, W. D. (1992). *Nonsampling error in surveys*. New York: John Wiley.

3

Sampling

How well a sample represents a population depends on the sample frame, the sample size, and the specific design of selection procedures. If probability sampling procedures are used, the precision of sample estimates can be calculated. This chapter describes various sampling procedures and their effects on the representativeness and precision of sample estimates. Two of the most common ways of sampling populations, area probability and random-digit-dialing samples, are described in some detail.

There are occasions when the goal of information gathering is not to generate statistics about a population but to describe a set of people in a more general way. Journalists, people developing products, political leaders, and others sometimes just want a sense of people's feelings without great concern about numerical precision. Researchers do pilot studies to measure the range of ideas or opinions that people have or the way that variables seem to hang together. For these purposes, people who are readily available (friends, coworkers) or people who volunteer (magazine survey respondents, people who call talk shows) may be useful. Not every effort to gather information requires a strict probability sample survey. For the majority of occasions when surveys are undertaken, however, the goal is to develop statistics about a population. This chapter is about sampling when the goal is to produce numbers that can be subjected appropriately to the variety of statistical techniques available to social scientists. Although many of the same general principles apply to any sampling problem, the chapter focuses on sampling people.

The way to evaluate a sample is not by the results, the characteristics of the sample, but by examining the process by which it was selected. There are three key aspects of sample selection:

1. The sample frame is the set of people that has a chance to be selected, given the sampling approach that is chosen. Statistically speaking, a sample only can be representative of the population included in the sample frame. One design issue is how well the sample frame corresponds to the population a researcher wants to describe.

2. Probability sampling procedures must be used to designate individual units for inclusion in a sample. Each person must have a known chance of

selection set by the sampling procedure. If researcher discretion or respondent characteristics such as respondent availability or initiative affect the chances of selection, there is no statistical basis for evaluating how well or how poorly the sample represents the population; commonly used approaches to calculating confidence intervals around sample estimates are not applicable.

3. The details of the sample design, its size and the specific procedures used for selecting units, will influence the precision of sample estimates, that is, how closely a sample is likely to approximate the characteristics of the whole population.

These details of the sampling process, along with the rate at which information actually is obtained from those selected, constitute the facts needed to evaluate a survey sample.

Response rates are discussed in Chapter 4, which also includes a brief discussion of quota sampling, a common modification of probability sampling that yields *nonprobability* samples. In this chapter, sampling frames and probability sampling procedures are discussed. Several of the most common practical strategies for sampling people are described. Interested readers will find much more information on sampling in Kish (1965), Sudman (1976), Kalton (1983), Groves (1989), Henry (1990), and Lohr (1998). Researchers planning to carry out a survey almost always would be well advised to obtain the help of a sampling statistician. This chapter, however, is intended to familiarize readers with the issues to which they should attend, and that they will likely encounter, when evaluating the sampling done for a survey.

THE SAMPLE FRAME

Any sample selection procedure will give some individuals a chance to be included in the sample while excluding others. Those people who have a chance of being included among those selected constitute the sample frame. The first step in evaluating the quality of a sample is to define the sample frame. Most sampling schemes fall into three general classes:

1. Sampling is done from a more or less complete list of individuals in the population to be studied.

2. Sampling is done from a set of people who go somewhere or do something that enables them to be sampled (e.g., patients who received medical care from a physician, or people who attended a meeting). In these cases, there

is not an advance list from which sampling occurs; the creation of the list and the process of sampling may occur simultaneously.

3. Sampling is done in two or more stages, with the first stage involving sampling something other than the individuals finally to be selected. In one or more steps, these primary units are sampled, and eventually a list of individuals (or other sampling units) is created, from which a final sample selection is made. One of the most common such sampling schemes is to select housing units, with no prior information about who lives in them, as a first stage of selecting a sample of people living in those housing units. These multistage procedures will be described in more detail later in this chapter.

There are three characteristics of a sample frame that a researcher should evaluate:

1. *Comprehensiveness*, that is, how completely it covers the target population.

2. Whether or not a person's *probability of selection* can be calculated.

3. *Efficiency*, or the rate at which members of the target population can be found among those in the frame.

Comprehensiveness. A sample can only be representative of the sample frame, that is, the population that actually had a chance to be selected. Most sampling approaches leave out at least a few people from the population the researcher wants to study. For example, household-based samples exclude people who live in group quarters such as dormitories, prisons, and nursing homes, as well as those who are homeless. Available general lists, such as those of people with driver's licenses, registered voters, and homeowners, are even more exclusive. Although they cover large segments of some populations, they also omit major segments with distinctive characteristics. As a specific example, published telephone directories omit those without landline telephones, those who have requested that their numbers not be published, and those who have been assigned a telephone number since the most recent directory was published. In some central cities, such exclusions amount to almost 50% of all households. In such cities, a sample drawn from a telephone directory would be representative of only about half the population, and the half that is represented could easily be expected to differ in many ways from the half that is not.

A growing threat to telephone surveys is the increase of cell phone use. Most telephone surveys have depended on sampling telephone numbers that can be linked to households. Households that are not served by any "landline" are excluded using the techniques most often used to draw samples for telephone surveys. Those households which are served only by cell phones are therefore left out of such samples (Blumberg, Lake, & Cynamon, 2006).

E-mail addresses provide another good example. There are some populations, such as those in business or school settings, that have virtually universal access to e-mail, and more or less complete lists of the addresses of these populations are likely to be available. On the other hand, as an approach to sampling households in the general population, sampling those with e-mail addresses leaves out many people and produces a sample that is very different from the population as a whole in many important ways. Moreover, there is not currently a way to create a good list of all or even most of those who have e-mail addresses.

Two recent innovations, spurred by the desire to conduct survey via the Internet, deserve mentioning. First, large numbers of people have been recruited via the Internet to participate in surveys and other research studies. These people fill out initial baseline questionnaires covering a large number of characteristics. The answers to these questions can then be used to "create" a sample from the total pool of volunteers that roughly matches those of the whole population a researcher wants to study. When such a "sample" is surveyed, the results may or may not yield accurate information about the whole population. Obviously, no one is included in such a sample who does not use the Internet and is not interested in volunteering to be in the surveys. Often, the same people participate in numerous surveys, thereby further raising questions about how well the respondents typify the general population (Couper, 2007).

In an effort to address some of those concerns, another approach is to carry out a telephone survey to recruit a pool of volunteers for Internet surveys. Those without access to computers may be given a computer to use. Even with those efforts, the "sample frame" consists of that subset of the population that lives in a household with telephone service and agrees to be part of a pool for research studies. From a statistical perspective, statistics based on samples from that pool do not necessarily apply to the balance of the population. Rather, in both of the examples above, those responding to a survey can only be said to be representative of the populations that volunteered or agreed to be on these lists (Couper, 2007). The extent to which they are like the rest of the population must be evaluated independently of the sampling process.

A key part of evaluating any sampling scheme is determining the percentage of the population one wants to describe that has a chance of being selected and the extent to which those excluded are distinctive. Very often a researcher must make a choice between an easier or less expensive way of sampling a population that leaves out some people and a more expensive strategy that is also more comprehensive. If a researcher is considering sampling from a list, it is particularly important to evaluate the list to find out in detail how it was compiled, how and when additions and deletions are made, and the number and characteristics of people likely to be left off the list.

Probability of selection. Is it possible to calculate the probability of selection of each person sampled? A procedure that samples records of visits to a doctor over a year will give individuals who visit the doctor numerous times a higher chance of selection than those who see the doctor only once. It is not necessary that a sampling scheme give every member of the sampling frame the same chance of selection, as would be the case if each individual appeared once and only once on a list. It is essential, however, that the researcher be able to find out the probability of selection for each individual selected. This may be done at the time of sample selection by examination of the list. It also may be possible to find out the probability of selection at the time of data collection.

In the above example of sampling patients by sampling doctor visits, if the researcher asks selected patients the number of visits to the physician they had in a year or if the researcher could have access to selected patients' medical records, it would be possible to adjust the data at the time of analysis to take into account the different chances of selection. If it is not possible to know the probability of selection of each selected individual, however, it is not possible to estimate accurately the relationship between the sample statistics and the population from which it was drawn.

"Quota samples," discussed near the end of Chapter 4, are another common example of using procedures for which the probability of selection cannot be calculated.

Efficiency. In some cases, sampling frames include units that are not members of the target population the researcher wants to sample. Assuming that eligible persons can be identified at the point of data collection, being too comprehensive is not a problem. Hence a perfectly appropriate way to sample elderly people living in households is to draw a sample of all households, find out if there are elderly persons living in selected households, then exclude those households with no elderly residents. Random-digit dialing samples select telephone numbers (many of which are not in use) as a way of sampling housing units with telephones. The only question about such designs is whether or not they are cost effective.

Because the ability to generalize from a sample is limited by the sample frame, when reporting results the researcher must tell readers who was or was not given a chance to be selected and, to the extent that it is known, how those omitted were distinctive.

SELECTING A ONE-STAGE SAMPLE

Once a researcher has made a decision about a sample frame or approach to getting a sample, the next question is specifically how to select the individual units to be included. In the next few sections, the various ways that samplers typically draw samples are discussed.

Simple Random Sampling

Simple random sampling is, in a sense, the prototype of population sampling. The most basic ways of calculating statistics about samples assume that a simple random sample was drawn. Simple random sampling approximates drawing a sample out of a hat: Members of a population are selected one at a time, independent of one another and without replacement; once a unit is selected, it has no further chance to be selected.

Operationally, drawing a simple random sample requires a numbered list of the population. For simplicity, assume that each person in the population appears once and only once. If there were 8,500 people on a list, and the goal was to select a simple random sample of 100, the procedure would be straightforward. People on the list would be numbered from 1 to 8,500. Then a computer, a table of random numbers, or some other generator of random numbers would be used to produce 100 different numbers within the same range. The individuals corresponding to the 100 numbers chosen would constitute a simple random sample of that population of 8,500. If the list is in a computerized data file, randomizing the ordering of the list, then choosing the first 100 people on the reordered list, would produce an equivalent result.

Systematic Samples

Unless a list is short, has all units prenumbered, or is computerized so that it can be numbered easily, drawing a simple random sample as described above can be laborious. In such situations, there is a way to use a variation called systematic sampling that will have precision equivalent to a simple random sample and can be mechanically easier to create. Moreover, the benefits of stratification (discussed in the next section) can be accomplished more easily through systematic sampling.

When drawing a systematic sample from a list, the researcher first determines the number of entries on the list and the number of elements from the list that are to be selected. Dividing the latter by the former will produce a fraction. Thus, if there are 8,500 people on a list and a sample of 100 is required, 100/8,500 of the list (i.e., 1 out of every 85 persons) is to be included in the sample. In order to select a systematic sample, a start point is designated by choosing a random number that falls within the sampling interval, in this example, any number from 1 to 85. The randomized start ensures that it is a chance selection process. Starting with the person in the randomly selected position, the researcher proceeds to take every 85th person on the list.

Most statistics books warn against systematic samples if a list is ordered by some characteristic, or has a recurring pattern, that will differentially affect the sample depending on the random start. As an extreme example, if members of a male-female couples club were listed with the male partner always listed first, any even number interval would produce a systematic sample that consisted of only one gender even though the club as a whole is evenly divided by gender. It definitely is important to examine a potential sample frame from the perspective of whether or not there is any reason to think that the sample resulting from one random start will be systematically different from those resulting from other starts in ways that will affect the survey results. In practice, most lists or sample frames do not pose any problems for systematic sampling. When they do, by either reordering the lists or adjusting the selection intervals, it almost always is possible to design a systematic sampling strategy that is at least equivalent to a simple random sample.

Stratified Samples

When a simple random sample is drawn, each new selection is independent, unaffected by any selections that came before. As a result of this process, any of the characteristics of the sample may, by chance, differ somewhat from the population from which it is drawn. Generally, little is known about the characteristics of individual population members before data collection. It is not uncommon, however, for at least a few characteristics of a population to be identifiable at the time of sampling. When that is the case, there is the possibility of structuring the sampling process to reduce the normal sampling variation, thereby producing a sample that is more likely to look like the total population than a simple random sample. The process by which this is done is called stratification.

For example, suppose one had a list of college students. The list is arranged alphabetically. Members of different classes are mixed throughout the list. If the list identifies the particular class to which a student belongs, it would be possible to rearrange the list to put freshmen first, then sophomores, then juniors, and finally seniors, with all classes grouped together. If the sampling design calls for selecting a sample of 1 in 10 of the members on the list, the rearrangement would ensure that exactly 1/10 of the freshmen were selected, 1/10 of the sophomores, and so forth. On the other hand, if either a simple random sample or a systematic sample was selected from the original alphabetical list, the proportion of the sample in the freshman year would be subject to normal sampling variability and could be slightly higher or lower than was the case for the population. Stratifying in advance ensures that the sample will have exactly the same proportions in each class as the whole population.

Consider the task of estimating the average age of the student body. The class in which a student is a member almost certainly is correlated with age. Although there still will be some variability in sample estimates because of the sampling procedure, structuring the representation of classes in the sampling frame also will constrain the extent to which the average age of the sample will differ by chance from the population as a whole.

Almost all samples of populations of geographic areas are stratified by some regional variable so that they will be distributed in the same way as the population as a whole. National samples typically are stratified by region of the country and also by urban, suburban, and rural locations. Stratification only increases the precision of estimates of variables that are related to the stratification variables. Because some degree of stratification is relatively simple to accomplish, however, and because it never hurts the precision of sample estimates (as long as the probability of selection is the same across all strata), it usually is a desirable feature of a sample design.

Different Probabilities of Selection

Sometimes stratification is used as a first step to vary the rates of selection of various population subgroups. When probabilities of selection are constant across strata, a group that constitutes 10% of a population will constitute about 10% of a selected sample. If a researcher wanted a sample of at least 100 from a population subgroup that constituted 10% of the population, a simple random sampling approach would require an overall sample of 1,000. Moreover, if the researcher decided to increase the sample size of that subgroup to 150, this would entail taking an additional 500 sample members into the sample, bringing the total to 1,500, so that 10% of the sample would equal 150.

Obviously, there are occasions when increasing a sample in this way is not very cost effective. In the latter example, if the researcher is satisfied with the size of the samples of other groups, the design adds 450 unwanted interviews in order to add 50 interviews that are wanted. In some cases, therefore, an appropriate design is to select some subgroup at a higher rate than the rest of the population.

As an example, suppose that a researcher wished to compare male and female students, with a minimum of 200 male respondents, at a particular college where only 20% of the students are male. Thus a sample of 500 students would include 100 male students. If male students could be identified in advance, however, one could select male students at twice the rate at which female students were selected. In this way, rather than adding 500 interviews to increase the sample by 100 males, an additional 100 interviews over the basic sample of 500 would produce a total of about 200 interviews with males. Thus, when making male-female comparisons, one would have the precision provided by samples of 200 male respondents and 400 female respondents. To combine these samples, the researcher would have to give male respondents a weight of half that given to females to compensate for the fact that they were sampled at twice the rate of the rest of the population. (See Chapter 10 for more details about weighting.)

Even if individual members of a subgroup of interest cannot be identified with certainty in advance of sampling, sometimes the basic approach outlined above can be applied. For instance, it is most unusual to have a list of housing units that identifies the race of occupants in advance of contact. It is not uncommon, however, for Asian families to be more concentrated in some neighborhood areas than others. In that instance, a researcher may be able to sample households in areas that are predominantly Asian at a higher than average rate to increase the number of Asian respondents. Again, when any group is given a chance of selection different from other members of the population, appropriate compensatory weighting is required in order to generate accurate population statistics for the combined or total sample.

A third approach is to adjust the chance of selection based on information gathered after making contact with potential respondents. Going back to the college student survey, if student gender could not be ascertained in advance, the researchers could select an initial sample of 1,000 students, have interviewers ascertain the gender of each student, then have them conduct a complete interview with all selected male students (200) but only half of the female students they identified (400). The result would be exactly the same as with the approach described above.

Finally, one other technical reason for using different probabilities of selection by stratum should be mentioned. If what is being measured is much more variable in one group than in another, it may help the precision of the resulting overall estimate to oversample the group with the high level of variability. Groves (1989) provides a good description of the rationale and how to assess the efficiency of such designs.

MULTISTAGE SAMPLING

When there is no adequate list of the individuals in a population and no way to get at the population directly, multistage sampling provides a useful approach. In the absence of a direct sampling source, a strategy is needed for linking population members to some kind of grouping that can be sampled. These groupings can be sampled as a first stage. Lists then are made of individual members of selected groups, with possibly a further selection from the created list at the second (or later) stage of sampling. In sampling terminology, the groupings in the last stage of a sample design are usually referred to as "clusters." The following section illustrates the general strategy for multistage sampling by describing its use in three of the most common types of situations in which lists of all individuals in the target population are not available.

Sampling Students From Schools

If one wanted to draw a sample of all students enrolled in the public schools of a particular city, it would not be surprising to find that there was not a single complete list of such individuals. There is, however, a sample frame that enables one to get at and include all the students in the desired population: namely, the list of all the public schools in that city. Because every individual in the study population can be attached to one and only one of those units, a perfectly acceptable sample of students can be selected using a two-stage strategy: first selecting schools (i.e., the clusters) and then selecting students from within those schools.

Assume the following data:

There are 20,000 students in a city with 40 schools

Desired sample = 2,000 = 1/10 of students

Four different designs or approaches to sampling are presented below. Each would yield a probability sample of 2,000 students.

The four approaches listed all yield samples of 2,000; all give each student in the city an equal (1 in 10) chance of selection. The difference is that from top to bottom, the designs are increasingly less expensive; lists have to be collected from fewer schools, and fewer schools need to be visited. At the same time, the precision of each sample is likely to decline as fewer schools are sampled and more students are sampled per school. The effect of this and other multistage designs on the precision of sample estimates is discussed in more detail in a later section of this chapter.

	Probability of Selection at Stage 1 (schools)	×	Probability of Selection at Stage 2 (students in selected schools)	=	Overall Probability of Selection
(a) Select all schools, list all students, and select 1/10 students in each school	1/1	×	1/10	=	1/10
(b) Select 1/2 of the schools, then select 1/5 of all students in them	1/2	×	1/5	=	1/10
(c) Select 1/5 of the schools, then select 1/2 of all students in them	1/5	×	1/2	=	1/10
(d) Select 1/10 schools, then collect information about all students in them	1/10	×	1/1	=	1/10

Area Probability Sampling

Area probability sampling is one of the most generally useful multistage strategies because of its wide applicability. It can be used to sample any population that can be defined geographically, for example, the people living in a neighborhood, a city, a state, or a country. The basic approach is to divide the total target land area into exhaustive, mutually exclusive subareas with identifiable boundaries. These subareas are the clusters. A sample of subareas is drawn. A list then is made of housing units in selected subareas, and a sample of listed units is drawn. As a final stage, all people in selected housing units may be included in the sample, or they may be listed and sampled as well.

This approach will work for jungles, deserts, sparsely populated rural areas, or downtown areas in central cities. The specific steps to drawing such a sample can be very complicated. The basic principles, however, can be illustrated by describing how one could sample the population of a city using city blocks as the primary subarea units to be selected at the first stage of sampling.

Assume the following data:
  A city consists of 400 blocks
  20,000 housing units are located on these blocks
  Desired sample = 2,000 housing units = 1/10 of all housing units
  Given this information, a sample of households could be selected using
a strategy parallel to the above selection of students. In the first stage of
sampling, blocks (i.e., the clusters) are selected. During the second stage, all
housing units on selected blocks are listed and a sample is selected from the
lists. Two approaches to selecting housing units are as follows:

	Probability of Selection Stage 1 (blocks)	×	Probability of Selection at Stage 2 (housing units in selected blocks)	=	Overall Probability of Selection
(a) Select 80 blocks (1/5), then take 1/2 of units on those blocks	1/5	×	1/2	=	1/10
(b) Select 40 blocks (1/10), then take all units on those blocks	1/10	×	1/1	=	1/10

  Parallel to the school example, the first approach, involving more blocks, is
more expensive than the second; it also is likely to produce more precise sample estimates for a sample of a given size.
  None of the above sample schemes takes into account the size of the Stage 1
groupings (i.e., the size of the blocks or schools). Big schools and big blocks
are selected at the same rates as small ones. If a fixed fraction of each selected
group is to be taken at the last stage, there will be more interviews taken from
selected big schools or big blocks than from small ones; the size of the samples
(cluster sizes) taken at Stage 2 will be very divergent.
  If there is information available about the size of the Stage 1 groups, it is usually good to use it. Sample designs tend to provide more precise estimates if the
number of units selected at the final step of selection is approximately equal in
all clusters. Other advantages of such designs are that sampling errors are easier
to calculate and the total size of the sample is more predictable. To produce
equal-sized clusters, Stage 1 units should be sampled proportionate to their size.
  The following example shows how blocks could be sampled proportionate
to their size as the first stage of an area probability approach to sampling housing

units (apartments or single family houses). The same approach could be applied to the school example above, treating schools in a way analogous to blocks in the following process.

1. Decide how many housing units are to be selected at the last stage of sampling—the average cluster size. Let us choose 10, for example.

2. Make an estimate of the number of housing units in each Stage 1 unit (block).

3. Order the blocks so that geographically adjacent or otherwise similar blocks are contiguous. This effectively stratifies the sampling to improve the samples, as discussed above.

4. Create an estimated cumulative count across all blocks of housing units. A table like the one below will result.

Block Number	Estimated Housing Units	Cumulative Housing Units	Hits (Random Start = 70; Interval = 100 HUs)
1	43	43	–
2	87	130	70
3	99	229	170
4	27	256	–
5	15	271	270

Determine the interval between clusters. If we want to select 1 in 10 housing units and a cluster of about 10 on each selected block, we need an interval of 100 housing units between clusters. Put another way, instead of taking 1 house at an interval of every 10 houses, we take 10 houses at an interval of every 100 houses; the rate is the same, but the pattern is "clustered."

After first choosing a random number from 1 to 100 (the interval in the example) as a starting point, we proceed systematically through the cumulative count, designating the primary units (or blocks) hit in this first stage of selection. In the example, the random start chosen (70) missed block 1 (though 43 times in 100 it would have been hit); the 70th housing unit was in block 2; the 170th housing unit was in block 3; and the 270th housing unit was located in block 5.

A list then is made of the housing units on the selected blocks (2, 3, and 5), usually by sending a person to visit the blocks. The next step is to select housing units from those lists. If we were sure the estimates of the sizes of blocks were accurate, we could simply select 10 housing units from each selected block, using either simple random or systematic sampling; a systematic sample would usually be best because it would distribute the chosen units around the block.

It is common for estimates of the size of stage 1 units such as blocks to be somewhat in error. We can correct for such errors by calculating the rate at which housing units are to be selected from blocks as:

(On block 2)

$$\frac{\text{Rate of HU}}{\text{selection on block}} = \frac{\text{Avg. cluster size}}{\text{Estimated HUs on block}} = \frac{10}{87} = \frac{1}{8.7}$$

In our example, we would take 1 per 8.7 housing units on block 2, 1 per 9.9 housing units on block 3, and 1 per 1.5 housing units on block 5. If a block is bigger than expected (e.g., because of new construction), more than 10 housing units will be drawn; if it is smaller than expected (e.g., because of demolition), fewer than 10 housing units will be drawn. If it is exactly what we expected (e.g., 87 housing units on block 2), we take 10 housing units (87) 8.7 = 10). In this way, the procedure is self-correcting for errors in initial estimates of block size, while maintaining the same chance of selection for housing units on all blocks. No matter the estimated or actual size of the block, the chance of any housing unit being selected is 1 in 10.

The area probability sample approach can be used to sample any geographically defined population. Although the steps are more complicated as the area gets bigger, the approach is the same. The key steps to remember are the following:

• All areas must be given some chance of selection. Combine areas where no units are expected with adjacent areas to ensure a chance of selection; new construction may have occurred or estimates may be wrong.

• The probability of selecting a block (or other land area) times the probability of selecting a housing unit from a selected block should be constant across all blocks.

Finally, even careful field listers will miss some housing units. Therefore, it is good practice to include checks for missed units at the time of data collection.

Random-Digit Dialing

Random-digit dialing (RDD) provides an alternative way to draw a sample of housing units in order to sample the people in those households. Suppose the 20,000 housing units in the above example are covered by six telephone exchanges. One could draw a probability sample of 10% of the housing units that have telephones as follows:

1. There is a total of 60,000 possible telephone numbers in those 6 exchanges (10,000 per exchange). Select 6,000 of those numbers (i.e., 10%), drawing 1,000 randomly generated, four-digit numbers per exchange.

2. Dial all 6,000 numbers. Not all the numbers will be household numbers; in fact, many of the numbers will not be working, will be disconnected or temporarily not in service, or will be businesses. Because 10% of all possible telephone numbers that could serve the area have been called, about 10% of all the households with telephones in that area will be reached by calling the sample of numbers.

This is the basic random-digit-dialing approach to sampling. The obvious disadvantage of this approach is the large number of unfruitful calls. Nationally, fewer than 25% of possible numbers are associated with residential housing units; the rate is about 30% in urban areas and about 10% in rural areas. Waksberg (1978) developed a method of taking advantage of the fact that telephone numbers are assigned in groups. Each group of 100 telephone numbers is defined by a three-digit area code, a three-digit exchange, and two additional numbers (area code–123–45XX). By carrying out an initial screening of numbers by calling one random number in a sample of groups, then calling additional random numbers only within the groups of numbers where a residential number was found, the rate of hitting housing units can be raised to more than 50%. In this design, the groups of 100 telephone numbers are the clusters.

In recent years, most survey organizations have begun using a list-assisted approach to RDD. With the advancement of computer technology, companies can compile computerized versions of telephone listings. These computerized phone books are updated every 3 months. Once all these books are in a computer file, a search can yield all clusters (area code– 123–45XX) that have at least one published residential telephone number. These companies can then produce a sample frame of all possible telephone numbers in clusters that have at least one published residential telephone number. Sampling can now be carried out using this sample frame. This approach has two distinct advantages. The first is that the initial screening of telephone numbers required by the Waksberg method is no longer needed. The construction of the sample frame has already accomplished this. The second advantage is that the sample selected using this frame is no longer clustered. By using all clusters that contain residential telephone numbers as a sample frame, a simple or systematic random sample of telephone numbers can be drawn. This new approach to

RDD is more cost effective and efficient than its predecessors were. A limitation is that telephone numbers in clusters that have no listed residential numbers have no chance of selection. Brick, Waksberg, Kulp, and Starer (1995) have estimated that, on average, about 4% of households with telephone service in the United States are left out. Lepkowski (1988) provides a good summary of the various ways to sample telephone numbers in order to sample households.

The accumulation of lists of individuals and their characteristics has made possible some other efficiencies for telephone surveys. One comparatively simple advance is that reverse telephone directories can be used to tie addresses to some telephone numbers. One of the downsides of RDD is that households do not receive advance notice that an interviewer will be calling. Lists make it possible to sort selected numbers into groups (or strata) based on whether or not there is a known residential address associated with a number. Those for whom there is a known address can be sent an advance letter.

More elaborately, if there are lists of people who have known characteristics that are targeted for a survey—an age group, those living in a particular geographic area, people who gave to a particular charity—a stratum can be made of telephone numbers likely to connect to households that are being targeted. Numbers in the other strata or for which information is not available may be sampled at lower rates, thereby giving all households a known chance of selection but increasing the efficiency of the data collection by concentrating more effort on households likely to yield eligible respondents. Note that if the probabilities of selection are not the same for all respondents, weighting must be used at the analysis stage, as described in Chapter 10.

There are several additional issues to note about the random-digit-dialing approach to sampling. First, its value depends on the fact that most households have telephone service. Nationally, only about 5% of the households lack household service, but in some areas, particularly central cities or rural areas, the rate of omission may be greater than that. The growing use of individual cell phones has also posed a growing problem for RDD sampling. Most current RDD sampling focuses only on household service and avoids exchanges devoted to cell phone use. It is possible to sample from both kinds of services, but the complexity of sampling, data collection, and postsurvey weighting are greatly increased if cell phone numbers are included in the sample frames (Brick, Dipko, Presser, Tucker, & Yuan, 2006; Lavrakas, Shuttles, Steeh, & Fienberg, 2007).

To give one example of the complexity: RDD sampling uses area codes to target populations in defined geographic areas. However, cell phone numbers are much less tied to where people actually live. A survey based on cell phone area codes will reach some people who live outside the targeted geographic area and, worse, will omit those who live in the area but whose cell phones have distant area codes.

Like any particular sampling approach, RDD is not the best design for all surveys. Additional pros and cons will be discussed in Chapter 5. The introduction of RDD as one sampling option, however, has made a major contribution to expanding survey research capabilities in the last 30 years. With the longer-term impact of cell phones and response rate challenges (discussed in Chapter 5), the future use of RDD sampling remains to be seen.

Respondent Selection

Both area probability samples and RDD designate a sample of housing units. There is then the further question of who in the household should be interviewed.

The best decision depends on what kind of information is being gathered. In some studies, the information is being gathered about the household and about all the people in the household. If the information is commonly known and easy to report, perhaps any adult who is home can answer the questions. If the information is more specialized, the researcher may want to interview the household member who is most knowledgeable. For example, in the National Health Interview Survey, the person who "knows the most about the health of the family" is to be the respondent for questions that cover all family members.

There are, however, many things that an individual can report only for himself or herself. Researchers almost universally feel that no individual can report feelings, opinions, or knowledge for some other person. There are also many behaviors or experiences (e.g., what people eat or drink, what they have bought, what they have seen, or what they have been told) that usually can only be reported accurately by self-reporters.

When a study includes variables for which only self-reporting is appropriate, the sampling process must go beyond selecting households to sampling specific individuals within those households. One approach is to interview every eligible person in a household. (So there is no sampling at that stage.) Because of homogeneity within households, however, as well as concerns about one respondent influencing a later respondent's answers, it is more common to designate a single respondent per household. Obviously, taking the person who happens to answer the phone or the door would be a nonprobabilistic and potentially biased way of selecting individuals; interviewer discretion, respondent discretion, and availability (which is related to working status, lifestyle, and age) would all affect who turned out to be the respondent. The key principle of probability sampling is that selection is carried out through some chance or random procedure that designates specific people. The procedure for generating a probability selection of respondents within households involves three steps:

1. Ascertain how many people living in a household are eligible to be respondents (e.g., how many are 18 or older).
2. Number these in a consistent way in all households (e.g., order by decreasing age).
3. Have a procedure that objectively designates one person to be the respondent.

Kish (1949) created a detailed procedure for designating respondents using a set of randomized tables that still is used today. When interviewing is computer assisted, it is easy to have the computer select one of the eligible household members. The critical features of the procedure are that no discretion be involved and that all eligible people in selected households have a known (and nonzero) probability of selection. Groves and Lyberg (1988) review several strategies for simplifying respondent selection procedures.

One of the concerns about respondent selection procedures is that the initial interaction upon first contacting someone is critical to enlisting cooperation. If the respondent selection procedure is too cumbersome or feels intrusive, it may adversely affect the rate of response. Thus, there have been various efforts to find streamlined ways to sample adults in selected households.

One popular method is the "last birthday" method. The household contact is asked to identify the adult who last had a birthday, and that person is the designated respondent. In principle, this should be an unbiased way to select a respondent. In practice, it depends on the initial contact having information about all household members' birthdays.

Another relatively new approach keys selection to the person the interviewer first talks with. First, the number of eligible people in the household is determined. If there are two or more eligible, a randomized algorithm chooses either the initial informant at the appropriate rate or chooses among the "other" eligible adults (if there is more than one) (Rizzo, Brick, & Park, 2004).

However the respondent is chosen, when only one person is interviewed in a household, a differential rate of selection is introduced. If an adult lives in a one-adult household, he or she obviously will be the respondent if the household is selected. In contrast, an adult living in a three-adult household only will be the respondent one third of the time. Whenever an identifiable group is selected at a different rate from others, weights are needed so that oversampled people are not overrepresented in the sample statistics. In the example earlier in this chapter, when male students were selected at twice the rate of female students, their responses were weighted by one half so that their weighted proportion of the sample would be the same as in the population. The same general approach applies when one respondent is chosen from households with varying numbers of eligible people.

The simplest way to adjust for the effect of selecting one respondent per household is to weight each response by the number of eligible people in that household. Hence, if there are three adults, the weight is three; if there are two eligible adults, the weight is two; and if there is only one eligible adult, the weight is one. If a weighting scheme is correct, the probability of selection times the weight is the same for all respondents. (See Chapter 10.)

MAKING ESTIMATES FROM
SAMPLES AND SAMPLING ERRORS

The sampling strategies presented above were chosen because they are among the most commonly used and they illustrate the major sampling design options. A probability sampling scheme eventually will designate a specific set of households or individuals without researcher or respondent discretion. The basic tools available to the researcher are simple random and systematic sampling, which are modified by stratification, unequal rates of selection, and clustering. The choice of a sampling strategy rests in part on feasibility and costs; it also involves the precision of sample estimates. A major reason for using probability sampling methods is to permit use of a variety of statistical tools to estimate the precision of sample estimates. In this section, the calculation of such estimates and how they are affected by features of the sample design are discussed.

Researchers usually have no interest in the characteristics of a sample per se. The reason for collecting data about a sample is to reach conclusions about an entire population. The statistical and design issues in this chapter are considered in the context of how much confidence one can have that the characteristics of a sample accurately describe the population as a whole.

As described in Chapter 2, a way to think about sampling error is to think of the distribution of means one might get if many samples were drawn from the same population with the same procedure. Although some sources of error in surveys are biasing and produce systematically distorted figures, sampling error is a random (and hence not a systematically biasing) result of sampling. When probability procedures are used to select a sample, it is possible to calculate how much sample estimates will vary by chance because of sampling.

If an infinite number of samples are drawn, the sample estimates of descriptive statistics (e.g., means) will form a normal distribution around the true population value. The larger the size of the sample and the less the variance of what is being measured, the more tightly the sample estimates will bunch around the true population value, and the more accurate a sample-based estimate usually will be. This variation around the true value, stemming from the fact that by chance samples may differ from the population as a whole, is called "sampling error." Estimating the limits of the confidence one can have in a sample estimate, given normal chance sampling variability, is one important part of evaluating figures derived from surveys.

The design of sample selection (specifically, whether it involves stratification, clustering, or unequal probabilities of selection) affects the estimates of sampling error for a sample of a given size. The usual approach to describing sampling errors, however, is to calculate what they would be for a simple random sample, and then to calculate the effects of deviations from a simple random sampling design. Hence, the calculation of sampling errors for simple random samples is described first.

Sampling Errors for Simple Random Samples

This is not a textbook on sampling statistics. Estimating the amount of error one can expect from a particular sample design, however, is a basic part of the survey design process. Moreover, researchers routinely provide readers with guidelines regarding error attributable to sampling, guidelines that both the knowledgeable reader and the user of survey research data should know and understand. To this end, a sense of how sampling error is calculated is a necessary part of understanding the total survey process.

Although the same logic applies to all statistics calculated from a sample, the most common sample survey estimates are means or averages. The statistic most often used to describe sampling error is called the *standard error* (of a mean). *It is the standard deviation of the distribution of sample estimates of means that would be formed if an infinite number of samples of a given size were drawn.* When the value of a standard error has been estimated, one can say that 67% of the means of samples of a given size and design will fall within the range of ±1 standard error of the true population mean; 95% of such samples will fall within the range of ±2 standard errors. The latter figure (±2 standard errors) often is reported as the "confidence interval" around a sample estimate.

The estimation of the standard error of a mean is calculated from the variance and the size of the sample from which it was estimated:

$$SE = \sqrt{\frac{\text{Var}}{n}}$$

SE = standard error of a mean
Var = the variance (the sum of the squared deviations from the sample mean over n)
n = size of the sample

The most common kind of mean calculated from a sample survey is probably the percentage of a sample that has a certain characteristic or gives a certain response. It may be useful to show how a percentage is the mean of a two-value distribution.

A mean is an average. It is calculated as the sum of the values divided by the number of cases: $\Sigma x/n$. Now suppose there are only two values, 0 (no) and 1 (yes). There are 50 cases in a sample; 20 say "yes" when asked if they are married, and the rest say "no." If there are 20 "yes" and 30 "no" responses, calculate the mean as

$$\frac{\sum X}{n} = \frac{(20 \times 1 + 30 \times 0)}{50} = \frac{20}{50} = 0.40$$

A percentage statement, such as 40% of respondents are married, is just a statement about the mean of a 1/0 distribution; the mean is .40. The calculation of standard errors of percentage is facilitated by the fact that the variance of a percentage can be calculated readily as $p \times (1 - p)$, where p = percentage having a characteristic (e.g., the 40% married in the above example) and $(1 - p)$ is the percentage who lack the characteristic (e.g., the 60% not married).

We have already seen that the standard error of a mean is as follows:

$$SE = \sqrt{\frac{\text{Var}}{n}}$$

Because $p(1 - p)$ is the variance of a percentage,

$$SE = \sqrt{\frac{p(1-p)}{n}}$$

is the standard error of a percentage. In the previous example, with 40% of a sample of 50 persons being married, the standard error of that estimate would be as follows:

$$\text{SE} = \sqrt{\frac{p(1-p)}{n}} = \sqrt{\frac{0.40 \times 0.60}{50}} = \sqrt{\frac{0.24}{50}} = 0.07$$

Thus we would estimate that the probability is .67 (i.e., ±1 standard error from the sample mean) that the true population figure (the percentage of the whole population that is married) is between .33 and .47 (.40 ± .07). We are 95% confident that the true population figure lies within two standard errors of our sample mean, that is, between .26 and .54 (.40 ± .14).

Table 3.1 is a generalized table of sampling errors for samples of various sizes and for various percentages, provided that samples were selected as simple random samples. Each number in the table represents two standard errors of a percentage. Given knowledge (or an estimate) of the percentage of a sample that gives a particular answer, the table gives 95% confidence intervals for various sample sizes. In the example above, with 50 cases yielding a sample estimate of 40% married, the table reports a confidence interval near .14, as we calculated. If a sample of about 100 cases produced an estimate that 20% were married, the table says we can be 95% sure that the true figure is 20% ± 8 percentage points (i.e., 12% to 28%).

Several points about the table are worth noting. First, it can be seen that increasingly large samples always reduce sampling errors. Second, it also can be seen that adding a given number of cases to a sample reduces sampling error a great deal more when the sample is small than when it is comparatively large. For example, adding 50 cases to a sample of 50 produces a quite noticeable reduction in sampling error. Adding 50 cases to a sample of 500, however, produces a virtually unnoticeable improvement in the overall precision of sample estimates.

Third, it can be seen that the absolute size of the sampling error is greatest around percentages of .5 and decreases as the percentage of a sample having a characteristic approaches either zero or 100%. We have seen that standard errors are related directly to variances. The variance $p(1 - p)$ is smaller as the percentages get further from .5. When $p = 0.5$, $(0.5 \times 0.5) = 0.25$. When $p = 0.2$, $(0.2 \times 0.8) = 0.16$.

Fourth, Table 3.1 and the equations on which it is based apply to samples drawn with simple random sampling procedures. Most samples of general populations are not simple random samples. The extent to which the particular sample design will affect calculations of sampling error varies from design to design and for different variables in the same survey. More often than not,

TABLE 3.1
Confidence Ranges for Variablility Attributable to Sampling*

Percentage of Sample With Characteristic

Sample Size	5/95	10/90	20/80	30/70	50/50
35	7	10	14	15	17
50	6	8	11	13	14
75	5	7	9	11	12
100	4	6	8	9	10
200	3	4	6	6	7
300	3	3	5	5	6
500	2	3	4	4	4
1,000	1	2	3	3	3
1,500	1	2	2	2	2

NOTE: Chances are 95 in 100 that the real population figure lies in the range defined by ± number indicated in table, given the percentage of sample reporting the characteristic and the number of sample cases on which the percentage is based.

*This table describes variability attributable to sampling. Errors resulting from nonresponse or reporting errors are not reflected in this table. In addition, this table assumes a simple random sample. Estimates may be subject to more variability than this table indicates because of the sample design or the influence of interviewers on the answers they obtained; stratification might reduce the sampling errors below those indicated here.

Table 3.1 will constitute an underestimate of the sampling error for a general population sample.

Finally, it should be emphasized that the variability reflected in Table 3.1 describes potential for error that comes from the fact of sampling rather than collecting information about every individual in a population. The calculations do not include estimates of error from any other aspects of the survey process.

Effects of Other Sample Design Features

The preceding discussion describes the calculation of sampling errors for simple random samples. Estimates of sampling errors will be affected by different sampling procedures. Systematic sampling should produce sampling errors equivalent to simple random samples if there is no stratification. Stratified samples can produce sampling errors that are lower than those associated with simple random samples of the same size for variables that differ (on average) by stratum, if rates of selection are constant across strata. Unequal rates of selection (selecting subgroups in the population at different rates) are designed to increase the precision of estimates for oversampled subgroups, thus

(a) they generally will produce sampling errors for the whole sample that are higher than those associated with simple random samples of the same size, for variables that differ by stratum, except

(b) when oversampling is targeted at strata that have higher than average variances for some variable, the overall sampling errors for those variables will be lower than for a simple random sample of the same size.

Clustering will tend to produce sampling errors that are higher than those associated with simple random samples of the same size for variables that are more homogeneous within clusters than in the population as a whole. Also, the larger the size of the cluster at the last stage, the larger the impact on sampling errors will usually be.

It often is not easy to anticipate the effects of design features on the precision of estimates. Design effects differ from study to study and for different variables in the same survey. To illustrate, suppose every house on various selected blocks was the same with respect to type of construction and whether or not it was occupied by the owner. Once one respondent on a block reports he is a home owner, the additional interviews on that block would yield absolutely no new information about the rate of home ownership in the population as a whole. For that reason, whether the researcher took one interview per block or 20 interviews per block, the reliability of that estimate would be exactly the same, basically proportionate to the number of blocks from which any interviews at all were taken. At the other extreme, the height of adults is likely to vary as much within a block as it does throughout a city. If the respondents on a block are as heterogeneous as the population as a whole, clustering does not decrease the precision of estimates of height from a sample of a given size. Thus, one has to look at the nature of the clusters or strata and what estimates are to be made in order to evaluate the likely effect of clustering on sampling errors.

The effects of the sample design on sampling errors often are unappreciated. It is not uncommon to see reports of confidence intervals that assume simple random sampling when the design was clustered. It also is not a simple matter to anticipate the size of design effects beforehand. As noted, the effects of the sample design on sampling errors are different for every variable; their calculation is particularly complicated when a sample design has several deviations from simple random sampling, such as both clustering and stratification. Because the ability to calculate sampling errors is one of the principal strengths of the survey method, it is important that a statistician be involved in a survey with a complex sample design to ensure that sampling errors are calculated and reported appropriately. The problem of appropriately taking into account design features when estimating sampling errors has been greatly simplified by the fact that several available analysis packages will do those adjustments. (See Chapter 10.)

Finally, the appropriateness of any sample design feature can be evaluated only in the context of the overall survey objectives. Clustered designs are likely to save money both in sampling (listing) and in data collection. Moreover, it is common to find many variables for which clustering does not inflate the sampling errors very much. Oversampling one or more groups often is a cost-effective design. As with most issues discussed in this book, the important point is for a researcher to be aware of the potential costs and benefits of the options and to weigh them in the context of all the design options and the main purposes of the survey.

HOW BIG SHOULD A SAMPLE BE?

Of the many issues involved in sample design, one of the most common questions posed to a survey methodologist is how big a survey sample should be. Before providing an approach to answering this question, perhaps it is appropriate to discuss three common but inappropriate ways of answering it.

One common misconception is that the adequacy of a sample depends heavily on the fraction of the population included in that sample—that somehow 1%, or 5%, or some other percentage of a population will make a sample credible. The estimates of sampling errors discussed above do not take into account the fraction of a population included in a sample. The sampling error estimates from the preceding equations and from Table 3.1 can be reduced by multiplying them by the value $(1 - f)$, where f = the fraction of the population included in a sample.

When one is sampling 10% or more of a population, this adjustment can have a discernible effect on sampling error estimates. The vast majority of survey samples, however, involve very small fractions of populations. In such instances, small increments in the fraction of the population included in a sample will have no effect on the ability of a researcher to generalize from a sample to a population.

The converse of this principle also should be noted. The size of the population from which a sample of a particular size is drawn has virtually no impact on how well that sample is likely to describe the population. A sample of 150 people will describe a population of 15,000 or 15 million with virtually the same degree of accuracy, assuming that all other aspects of the sample design and sampling procedures are the same. Compared to the total sample size and other design features such as clustering, the impact of the fraction of a population sampled on sampling errors is typically trivial. It is most unusual for it to be an important consideration when deciding on a sample size.

A second inappropriate approach to deciding on sample size is somewhat easier to understand. Some people have been exposed to so-called standard survey studies, and from these they have derived a typical or appropriate sample size. Thus some people will say that good national survey samples generally are 1,500, or that good community samples are 500. Of course, it is not foolish to look at what other competent researchers have considered to be adequate sample sizes of a particular population. The sample size decision, however, like most other design decisions, must be made on a case-by-case basis, with the researchers considering the variety of goals to be achieved by a particular study and taking into account numerous other aspects of the research design.

A third wrong approach to deciding on sample size is the most important one to address, for it can be found in many statistical textbooks. The approach goes like this: A researcher should decide how much margin of error he or she can tolerate or how much precision is required of estimates. Once one knows the need for precision, one simply uses a table such as Table 3.1, or appropriate variations thereon, to calculate the sample size needed to achieve the desired level of precision.

In some theoretical sense, there is nothing wrong with this approach. In practice, however, it provides little help to most researchers trying to design real studies. First, it is unusual to base a sample size decision on the need for precision of a single estimate. Most survey studies are designed to make numerous estimates, and the needed precision for these estimates is likely to vary.

In addition, it is unusual for a researcher to be able to specify a desired level of precision in more than the most general way. It is only the exception, rather than the common situation, when a specific acceptable margin for error can be specified in advance. Even in the latter case, the above approach implies that sampling error is the only or main source of error in a survey estimate. When a required level of precision from a sample survey is specified, it generally ignores the fact that there will be error from sources other than sampling. In such cases, the calculation of precision based on sampling error alone is an unrealistic oversimplification. Moreover, given fixed resources, increasing the sample size may even decrease precision by reducing resources devoted to response rates, question design, or the quality of data collection.

Estimates of sampling error, which are related to sample size, do play a role in analyses of how big a sample should be. This role, however, is complicated. The first prerequisite for determining a sample size is an analysis plan. The key component of that analysis plan usually is not an estimate of confidence intervals for the overall sample, but rather an outline of the subgroups within the total population for which separate estimates are required, together with some estimates of the fraction of the population that will fall into those subgroups. Typically, the design process moves quickly to identifying the smaller groups within the population for which figures are needed. The researcher then estimates how large a sample will be required in order to provide a minimally adequate sample of these small subgroups. Most sample size decisions do not focus on estimates for the total population; rather, they are concentrated on the minimum sample sizes that can be tolerated for the smallest subgroups of importance.

The process then turns to Table 3.1, not at the high end but at the low end of the sample size continuum. Are 50 observations adequate? If one studies Table 3.1, it can be seen that precision increases rather steadily up to sample sizes of 150 to 200. After that point, there is a much more modest gain to increasing sample size.

Like most decisions relating to research design, there is seldom a definitive answer about how large a sample should be for any given study. There are many ways to increase the reliability of survey estimates. Increasing sample size is one of them. Even if one cannot say that there is a single right answer, however, it can be said that there are three approaches to deciding on sample size that are inadequate. Specifying a fraction of the population to be included in the sample is never the right way to decide on a sample size. Sampling errors primarily depend on sample size, not on the proportion of the population in a sample. Saying that a particular sample size is the usual or typical approach to studying a population also is virtually always the wrong approach. An analysis plan that addresses the study's goals is the critical first step. Finally, it is very rare that calculating a desired confidence interval for one variable for an entire population is the determining calculation in how big a sample should be.

SAMPLING ERROR AS A COMPONENT
OF TOTAL SURVEY ERROR

The sampling process can affect the quality of survey estimates in three different ways:

- If the sample frame excludes some people whom we want to describe, sample estimates will be biased to the extent that those omitted differ from those included.

• If the sampling process is not probabilistic, the relationship between the sample and those sampled is problematic. One can argue for the credibility of a sample on grounds other than the sampling process; however, there is no statistical basis for saying a sample is representative of the sampled population unless the sampling process gives each person selected a known probability of selection.

• The size and design of a probability sample, together with the distribution of what is being estimated, determine the size of the sampling errors, that is, the chance variations that occur because of collecting data about only a sample of a population.

Often sampling errors are presented in ways that imply they are the only source of unreliability in survey estimates. For surveys that use large samples, other sources of error are likely to be more important. A main theme of this book is that nonsampling errors warrant as much attention as sampling errors. Also, it is not uncommon to see sampling errors reported that assume simple random sampling procedures when the sample design involved clusters, or even when it was not a probability sample at all. In these ways, ironically, estimates of sampling errors can mislead readers about the precision or accuracy of sample estimates.

Sampling and analyzing data from a sample can be fairly straightforward if a good list is used as a sampling frame, if a simple random or systematic sampling scheme is used, and if all respondents are selected at the same rate. With such a design, Table 3.1 and the equations on which it is based will provide good estimates of sampling errors. Even with such straightforward designs, however, researchers need to consider all sources of error, including the sample frame, nonresponse, and response errors (all discussed in subsequent chapters) when evaluating the precision of survey estimates. Moreover, when there are doubts about the best way to sample, or when there are deviations from simple random sampling, it is virtually essential to involve a sampling specialist both to design an appropriate sampling plan and to analyze results properly from a complex sample design.

EXERCISES

1. In order to grasp the meaning of sampling error, repeated systematic samples of the same size (with different random starts) can be drawn from the same list (e.g., a telephone directory). The proportions of those samples having some characteristic (e.g., a business listing) taken together will form

a distribution. That distribution will have a standard deviation that is about one half the entry in Table 3.1 for samples of the sizes drawn. It is also valuable to calculate several of the entries in Table 3.1 (i.e., for various sample sizes and proportions) to help understand how the numbers were derived.

2. What percentage of adults in the United States would you estimate:

    a. Have driver's licenses?

    b. Have listed telephone numbers?

    c. Are registered to vote?

    d. Have a personal e-mail address (not through their work)?

3. What are some likely differences between those who would be in those sample frames and those who would not?

4. Compared with simple random samples, do the following tend to increase, decrease, or have no effect on sampling errors?

    a. Clustering?

    b. Stratifying?

    c. Using a systematic sampling approach?

Further Readings

Kalton, G. (1983). *Introduction to survey sampling.* Beverly Hills, CA: Sage.
Kish, L. (1965). *Survey sampling.* New York: John Wiley.
Lohr, S. L. (1998). *Sampling design and analysis.* New York: Brooks/Cole.

4

Nonresponse

Implementing a Sample Design

Failure to collect data from a high percentage of those selected to be in a sample is a major potential source of survey error. Approaches to contacting respondents and enlisting cooperation for mail, telephone, Internet, and personal interview surveys are discussed. The biases associated with nonresponse are described, as are the disadvantages of strategies such as quota samples to avoid the effort required to obtain high response rates.

The idea of a probability sample of people is that every individual in the target population (or at least the sample frame) has a known chance to have data collected about him or her. A sampling procedure will designate a specific set of individuals (or units of some kind); the quality of sample data depends on how well those from whom data actually are collected reflect the total population with respect to the variables the survey is designed to describe. The procedures used to collect data are as important as the sample selection process in determining how well data from a sample describe a population.

Of course, the accuracy of any particular estimate from a survey depends on who provides an answer to a particular question. In every survey, there are some respondents who do not answer every question. Although nonresponse to individual questions is usually low, occasionally it can be high and can have a real effect on estimates. The focus of this chapter, however, is on those people who do not provide any data at all. (See Chapter 10 for further discussion of item nonresponse.)

There are three categories of those selected to be in a sample who do not actually provide data:

- those whom the data collection procedures do not reach, thereby not giving them a chance to answer questions
- those asked to provide data who refuse to do so
- those asked to provide data who are unable to perform the task required of them (e.g., people who are too ill to be interviewed, who do not speak the researcher's language, or whose reading and writing skills preclude their filling out self-administered questionnaires)

The procedures that a researcher decides to use can have a major influence on the percentage of a sample that actually provides information (i.e., the response rate) and the extent to which nonrespondents introduce bias into sample data. For the most part, the likely effect of nonresponse is to bias samples, that is, to make them systematically different from the population from which they were drawn, thereby producing potentially biased estimates. In this chapter, the effect of nonresponse on survey estimates and procedures for reducing nonresponse are discussed.

CALCULATING RESPONSE RATES

The response rate is a basic parameter for evaluating a data collection effort. It is simply the number of people who complete the survey divided by the number of people (or units) sampled. The denominator includes all people in the study population who were selected but did not respond for whatever reason: refusals, language problems, illness, or lack of availability.

Sometimes a sample design will involve screening to find members of a population to be studied. Screened units that do not include people in the study population do not enter the response rate calculation. Hence vacant houses, telephone numbers that are not working or that do not serve residential units, and households where no eligible person resides (e.g., households in which no elderly people live when one is drawing a sample of elderly persons) are omitted in calculating response rates. If there are some units for which information needed to determine eligibility is not obtained, however, the response rate is uncertain. The best approach in this situation is to calculate the response rates using conservative and liberal assumptions about the rate of eligibility of unscreened units and report the range, together with a best estimate.

Response rates usually are reported as the percentage of a selected sample from whom data were collected. A further calculation can sometimes be made of the fraction of the population represented in the sample. If the sample frame did not omit anyone in the study population, the response rate is the same as the percentage of the population represented in the sample. If only 95% of the population has a telephone, however, the best estimate of the percentage of the population represented in a sample is .95 times the response rate for a telephone survey.

It is important to know the details of the way response rates are calculated. Differences in the way they are calculated can make comparisons difficult or inappropriate. For example, some organizations report a "completion rate," the percentage of households *contacted* at which an interview was completed.

Such numbers will always be higher than the response rate outlined above, which includes selected uncontacted units in the denominator. A publication available from the American Association of Public Opinion Research (AAPOR) provides an excellent discussion of response rate calculations and how to report them (AAPOR, 2006).

BIAS ASSOCIATED WITH NONRESPONSE

The effect of nonresponse on survey estimates depends on the percentage not responding and the extent to which those not responding are biased—that is, systematically different from the whole population. If most of those selected provide data, sample estimates will be very good even if the nonrespondents are distinctive. For example, when the U.S. Bureau of the Census carries out the National Health Interview Survey, it is successful in completing interviews in over 90% of selected households. It is easy to show that even if the nonresponding 10% is very distinctive, the resulting samples are still very similar to the population as a whole.

The experience of the Bureau of the Census is extreme in the positive direction. At the other extreme, one occasionally will see reports of mail or Internet surveys in which 5% to 20% of the selected sample responded. In such instances, the final sample may have little relationship to the original sampling process; those responding essentially are self-selected. It is very unlikely that such procedures will provide any credible statistics about the characteristics of the population as a whole.

Response rates for most survey research projects lie somewhere between these two extremes. Response rates generally are higher in rural areas than they are in central cities. It also is easier to collect information from any responsible adult in a household than to obtain an interview with a specific designated respondent. Some subjects (e.g., health) may interest more people than other topics (e.g., economic behavior or public opinions). Moreover, survey organizations differ considerably in the extent to which they devote time and money to improving response rates.

There is no agreed-upon standard for a minimum acceptable response rate. The Office of Management and Budget of the federal government, which reviews surveys done under contract to the government, generally asks that procedures be likely to yield a response rate in excess of 80% and requires a nonresponse analysis if a survey does not meet this standard (OMB, 2006). In the United States, academic survey organizations sometimes are able to achieve response rates for designated adults in the 70% range for in-person surveys with general household samples. The General Social Survey conducted by the National Opinion Research Center is an example. Rates of response for surveys of central city samples or using random-digit dialed telephone samples are likely to be lower—often much lower.

The nature of bias associated with nonresponse differs somewhat among mail, telephone, and personal interview procedures. One generalization that seems to hold up for most mail surveys is that people who have a particular interest in the subject matter or the research itself are more likely to return mail questionnaires than those who are less interested (Groves et al., 2006). This means that mail surveys with low response rates may be biased significantly in ways that are related directly to the purposes of the research (e.g., Filion, 1975; Heberlein & Baumgartner, 1978; Jobber, 1984). For example, one study of those who did not return a mail questionnaire about health care experience, but who were later interviewed by phone, indicated that mail nonrespondents were younger, healthier, used fewer health services, and were more likely to be male than the mail respondents (Fowler et al., 2002). Gallagher, Fowler, and Stringfellow (2005) reported on another study in which health records were available on nonrespondents, enabling them to conclude that the early mail respondents were significantly different from later respondents in several ways highly relevant to the survey.

Another example of significant bias from low response to mail questionnaires is the oft-cited *Literary Digest* presidential poll in 1936, which managed to predict a victory for Alf Landon in an election that Franklin Roosevelt won by a political landslide. The story is told that a sample was drawn from telephone books, and Republicans (those in Landon's party) were more likely to have telephones in 1936. In addition, however, the *Literary Digest* survey in 1936 was a mail survey. Its failure also was one of nonresponse; only a minority of those asked to return questionnaires did so. As is typical of mail surveys, those who wanted the underdog to win, the Landon supporters, were particularly likely to want to express their views (Bryson, 1976; Converse, 1987).

Availability is a more important source of nonresponse for telephone and personal surveys than for mail surveys. It is obvious that if a data collection effort is carried out between 9:00 a.m. and 5:00 p.m. on Mondays through Fridays, the people who will be available to be interviewed will be distinctive. Of course, most survey organizations emphasize contacting household on evenings and weekends. Nonetheless, those most likely to be found at home are stay-at-home parents, unemployed persons, and retired people. They will tend not to have busy volunteer and social lives. They are more likely to be parents of small children. Large households are more likely to have someone at home than households with only one or two members.

Accessibility of a different kind also produces biases associated with nonresponse. National surveys using personal interview procedures almost always have lower response rates in central cities than in suburbs and rural areas. There are three main reasons for this. First, the rate of hard-to-find single individuals is higher in central cities. Second, an increasing fraction of individuals in central cities live in apartment buildings that have significant security features that make it hard for interviewers to gain direct access to residents. Third, there are more areas in central cities where visits at night are uncomfortable for interviewers; hence they may not give difficult-to-find people as good a chance to be found at home.

The continuing increase in central city populations and other broad social changes (more single-person households, fewer families with children, more women in the labor force) have made the achievement of high response rates harder during the past 20 years for both in-person and telephone surveys. Telephone survey response rates may also suffer from increased use of caller ID and the rise of cell phone use—both of which may have decreased the rates at which people answer their landline phones and can be exposed to the interviewers' introductions. De Leeuw and de Heer (2002) report trends for decline in response rates internationally, as well as in the United States. The relative roles of noncontact and refusals in nonresponse vary from country to country.

There is some evidence that telephone procedures may reduce the differential response rate between central cities and rural areas because it is possible to give more thorough coverage to urban households, to make contact with people in high-security buildings, and to make a large number of efforts to find single people at home. On the other hand, less-educated people seem less willing to be interviewed in a random-digit telephone procedure, as are those over 65 years of age. These biases are found less often in personal interview surveys. Groves and Kahn (1979), Cannell, Groves, Magilavy, Mathiowetz, and Miller (1987), Groves and Lyberg (1988), and Groves and Couper (1998) present good evaluations of the nonresponse biases in telephone surveys.

Finally, there is bias associated with people who are unable to be interviewed or to fill out a form. These persons usually compose a small fraction of a general population. Leaving out people who are in a hospital, however, may be a very important omission when trying to estimate health care utilization or expenditures. There also are neighborhood areas or groups where omitting people who do not speak English would be a significant factor. If special steps are not taken to collect data from a particular group, the sample estimates apply to a more restricted population: the population that actually had a chance to answer the questions or provide data, given the data collection procedures implemented.

Although there tend to be demographic differences between respondents and nonrespondents for interviewer-administered surveys, particularly for random-digit dialing based telephone surveys, the effect of nonresponse on survey estimates is less clear. Keeter, Miller, Kohut, Groves, and Presser (2000) report a careful comparison of results of two telephone surveys: one yielded a 36% response rate, the other a 60% response rate. With respect to the political and social attitudes that were the topics of the surveys, there were very few statistically significant differences between the two survey results. The researchers reported a replication of this study with similar results (Keeter, Kennedy, Dimock, Best, & Craighill, 2006).

However, these studies should not lead researchers to believe that nonresponse is not an important source of error. Groves (2006) reports on an analysis of response rates and nonresponse error. He studied over 200 estimates based on 30 surveys that used various modes of data collection. He found considerable evidence of error due to nonresponse. However, he reached two other important conclusions:

1. The response rate for a survey was not a very good predictor of nonresponse error. The correlation he reports between the two is .33.
2. One main reason for the comparatively low association is the variability within surveys in the amount of nonresponse error for different variables.

Thus, for any given survey, some estimates may be affected a lot by nonresponse while others are affected very little.

The key issue is the extent to which nonresponse is related to the estimates the survey is designed to make. Groves, Presser, and Dipko (2004) report experimental results that show that people with roles relevant to a survey topic (such as new parents asked to do a survey on child care) are more likely than average to respond. However, they also found that such identifiable role groups often were small and, hence, might not have a measurable effect on survey estimates. It seems reasonable, and is consistent with existing evidence, that respondent interest in the subject may play a bigger role in response to mail surveys than when an interviewer enlists cooperation.

Altogether, we have clear evidence that nonresponse can affect survey estimates, but we usually lack the information to reliably predict when, and how much, nonresponse will or will not affect survey estimates. Moreover, the effect of nonresponse on one variable can be very different than for others in the same survey.

Table 4.1 presents an example to help thinking about the potential effects of nonresponse on results. Suppose a sample of 100 is drawn, and 90 respond (response rate of 90%). Of those 90, 45 say "yes" to some question; the other 45 say "no." There are 10 people (the nonrespondents) whose views we do not know. If they all were "yeses," the true figure for the population would be 55% "yes." Thus, given:

Response rate = 90%
50% of respondents say "yes"

The actual percentage in the originally selected sample who would say "yes" if they responded could be no more than 55% and no less then 45%. The possible range for the example is given in the right-hand column of Table 4.1.

Table 4.2 works out this logic for a range of response rates. It can be seen that when response rates are low, the potential for error due to nonresponse is very large.

TABLE 4.1
Example of Potential Error Due to Nonresponse

	Responding* (Answers Known)**	Nonrespondents (Answers Unknown)	Total Sample (Possible Range of Answers if Everyone Responded)
Yes	45	0 to 10	45 to 55
No	45	0 to 10	45 to 55
Total	90	10	100

*If response rate was 90%.
**If 50% of respondents answered "yes."

TABLE 4.2
Range of Possible True Percentages When 50% of Sample Gives an Answer, by Response Rate

	When Response Rate Is:				
	90%	70%	50%	30%	10%
If 50% of those responding gave a particular answer, true value if everyone in sample responded could range from:	45%–55%	35%–65%	25%–75%	15%–85%	5%–95%

SOURCE: Adapted from table developed by Jack Elinson and Mitchell D. Elinson. Personal communication.

It may be instructive to compare the potential effects of nonresponse bias, such as those presented in Table 4.2, with the effects of sampling error presented in the preceding chapter (see Table 3.1). One usually does not know how biased nonresponse is, but it is seldom a good assumption that nonresponse is unbiased. Efforts to ensure that response rates reach a reasonable level and to avoid procedures that systematically produce differences between respondents and nonrespondents are important ways to build confidence in the accuracy of survey estimates.

REDUCING NONRESPONSE

Telephone or Personal Interview Surveys

Just as one can always say that a larger sample will be more reliable than a small sample, all other things being equal, one also can say that a survey with a higher response rate probably will produce a better and less biased sample than one that has more nonresponse. At the very least, given that nonresponse error is usually unmeasured, one can say that higher response rates increase the credibility of a survey's results. As with any design decision, a researcher must choose how much effort to invest in reducing nonresponse.

Two different problems must be addressed in order to achieve a high rate of response for telephone and personal surveys: gaining access to the selected individuals and enlisting their cooperation.

To reduce nonresponse resulting from lack of availability

- Make numerous calls, concentrating on evenings and weekends. The number needed depends on the setting. Six calls per household are probably a minimum in urban areas. For phone studies, more calls can be made cheaply, and many organizations use 10 as a minimum. Often, many more calls than 10 are made.

- Have interviewers with flexible schedules who can make appointments at any time that is convenient to respondents.

To enlist cooperation

- If possible, send an informative advance letter. It reassures some respondents, and interviewers feel more confident as well.

- Effectively and accurately present the purposes of the project. Make sure respondents know their help is important and how it will be useful.

- Make sure that respondents will not be threatened by the task or the uses to which the data will be put.
- Have effective interviewers. Make sure they know that the response rate is important. Identify interviewers who are having response rate problems quickly and either retrain or do not continue to use interviewers who are not effective.
- Teach interviewers to listen to respondents and tailor the interaction to the individual rather than following a largely scripted approach to introducing the survey.

Striking the right balance between persistence and responsiveness to reluctant respondents is not easy. Participation in surveys is voluntary, but reluctance to participate is often based on ignorance. Groves and Couper (1998) present useful analyses of the reasons for respondent reluctance to be interviewed.

It is appropriate to ask respondents to be informed about the purposes of a survey before refusing. Most surveys serve a useful purpose from some vantage point. When a person refuses, the resulting data will be less accurate. Interviewers should be required to make a good effort to get respondents to the point that they know what they are being asked to do and why. It also is reasonable routinely to ask people who initially refuse to reconsider. A significant percentage of refusals result from contacting the respondent at the wrong time rather than a fundamental unwillingness to be interviewed. Between one quarter and one third of people who initially refuse will agree to be interviewed when asked again at a later time.

The interview process is generally a positive experience for respondents. If a survey research project is being conducted by a responsible group, responses will be kept strictly confidential. Survey researchers routinely respect confidentiality with the same zealousness that psychiatrists and journalists protect their sources. Many survey research projects are serving some reasonable cause to which the majority of people would be willing to contribute. If the interviewer is willing to arrange an interview at the respondent's convenience, pressures for time should not be extraordinary for most respondents. Finally, most respondents report that being interviewed is pleasurable. People like to have an opportunity to talk about themselves to a good listener.

RDD poses particularly significant challenges for achieving good response rates. When list-assisted approaches are used to select the sample, letters can be sent to households for which addresses are known. However, even when that is done, the burden is on the interviewer to engage the person who answers the telephone. The first few sentences are critical to success. Also, because telephone contacts are used for many sales and fund-raising purposes, some people start out with a negative orientation to calls from strangers. In that context, even conscientious organizations sometimes achieve response rates in the 30% to 50% range—particularly when the subject of the survey is not immediately engaging. The difficulty of achieving high response rates is one of the intrinsic limits of RDD as a sampling approach.

Finally, it should be noted that cash payments to respondents in advance of interviews have been shown to increase response rates to both in-person and telephone interviews. Historically, payments have been used primarily for interview studies that made unusual demands on respondents, such as those that involve multiple interviews. However, recent research shows that there is an impact or response rates for one-time interviews as well (Groves & Couper, 1998; Singer, 2002; Singer, Van Hoewyk, Gebler, Raghunnathan, & McGanagle, 1999; Singer, Van Hoewyk, & Maher, 2000). The most important value of small prepayments is probably to get respondents' attention so they read the advance letter or listen to the interviewer's introduction. It also probably engenders some positive feelings and, in some, the sense that a positive gesture by the research team may warrant some reciprocal positive gesture—such as doing the interview. Another reason for considering financial incentives, in addition to their effects on the overall response rates, is that they may reduce the nonresponse bias resulting from those most interested in a topic being overrepresented in samples—by inducing some less interested people to respond who otherwise would not.

Mail Surveys

The problems of reducing nonresponse to mail surveys are somewhat different. Getting to the respondent, which is a critical part of telephone and personal surveys, is generally not an issue if the researcher has an accurate mailing address. Most people eventually come home to pick up their mail. Rather, the main difficulty is inducing respondents to perform the task of responding without the intervention of an interviewer.

Writing a letter is not a very effective way to convince a high percentage of people to do something. Personal contact is significantly more effective than a letter. There is a large body of literature on strategies designed to attempt to make a mail contact more effective. Does one print a questionnaire on colored paper or white paper? How much good does an impressive letterhead do? How about endorsements? What is the value of paying people? Some researchers send money along with the questionnaire, whereas others promise reimbursement if the questionnaire is returned. Should the respondent letter be signed in blue ink? Is a real stamp better than a postage-paid envelope?

Generally speaking, almost anything that makes a mail questionnaire look more professional, more personalized, or more attractive will have some positive effect on response rates. Tending to such details probably is worthwhile in the aggregate; Dillman (2007, 2008) reviews these issues well. It probably is also important to make the instrument easy to complete. More details about design are provided in Chapter 6, but there are three points worth mentioning here.

1. The layout should be clear so it is easy to see how to proceed.

2. The questions should be attractively spaced, easy to read, and uncluttered.

3. The response tasks should be easy to do. Do not ask respondents to provide written answers, except at their option. The response tasks should be to check a box, circle a number, or some other equally simple task.

Again, Dillman (2007, 2008) provides extensive guidance on the layout of self-administered instruments.

Several reviews of published studies indicate that prepayment to respondents of several dollars increases mail responses rates (Fox, Crask, & Kim, 1988; James & Bolstein, 1990). Almost all studies showed a benefit, even surveys of doctors (Berry & Kanouse, 1987). However, it is only advance payment that has been shown to affect responses. Delaying payments, offers to give money to charities, and enrollments in drawings have not been shown to increase response rates (Warriner, Goyder, Jersten, Hohner, & McSpurren, 1996). Finally, there is no question that the most important difference between good mail surveys and poor mail surveys is the extent to which researchers make repeated contact with nonrespondents. A reasonable sequence of events, such as that outlined by Dillman (2007), might include the following:

1. About 10 days after the initial mailing, mail all nonrespondents a reminder card, emphasizing the importance of the study and of a high rate of response.

2. About 10 days after the postcard is mailed, mail the remaining nonrespondents a letter again emphasizing the importance of a high rate of return and including another questionnaire for those who threw the first one away.

3. If the response rate is still not satisfactory, probably the best next step is to call nonrespondents on the telephone. If phone numbers are not available or

if the expense of telephone calls seems too great, additional persuasion letters, night telegraph letters, overnight delivery, or other follow-up procedures that stand out and seem important have been shown to be helpful.

With telephone follow-ups, of course, response rates will be higher than without them. If the researcher is persistent, and if it is a reasonably well-conceived and well-designed study, acceptable response rates can be obtained by mail. There are many examples of mail surveys achieving response rates as high or higher than other modes (e.g., Fowler, Roman, & Di, 1998).

If a researcher is going to recontact nonrespondents, the researcher must know who has not returned a questionnaire. The process need not be circuitous or complex. A simple identifying number can be written on the questionnaire or on the return envelope. It is good practice to tell people in the covering letter what the number is for.

Occasionally, a researcher may want to reassure respondents that they will not be identified. There is a simple alternative strategy that works very well and still permits follow-up. The respondent is sent a questionnaire that has no identifier on it. Attached to the questionnaire is a separate postcard that has a respondent identifier, as follows:

Dear Researcher, I am sending this postcard at the same time that I am putting my completed questionnaire in the mail. Since my questionnaire is completely anonymous, this postcard will tell you that you need not send me a further reminder to return the questionnaire.

This procedure maintains the respondent's anonymity, at the same time telling the researcher when someone has completed the questionnaire. Some might think that respondents simply would send back the postcard in order to avoid further reminders, but this seldom happens. The numbers of postcards and questionnaires returned almost always come out to be about the same. Sieber (1992) discusses a wider range of ways to collect data anonymously.

Internet Surveys

Although surveys on the Internet are comparatively new, so there is not the same body of experience that exists for mail and interview surveys, the dynamics and challenges seem likely to closely parallel those for mail surveys. The problem is to induce people to respond without the intervention of an interviewer.

There are two main ways that the Internet is used for surveys: respondents are asked to answer questions by replying to an e-mail questionnaire or they are asked to go to a Web site where a survey form is waiting to be completed. For a variety of reasons, using e-mail as a data collection approach is not a very good idea (see Chapter 5), and the use of the Internet for surveys is primarily about getting respondents to visit a survey site and fill out a questionnaire.

The most common way to ask people to complete an Internet survey is to send an e-mail invitation. As one might expect, this can produce widely varying results. Dillman (2007) reports a survey of faculty that obtained a response rate near 60%, nearly the same rate as they obtained in a parallel mail version of the same survey. Kaplovitz, Hadlock, and Levine (2004) report a similar experiment with students that obtained an Internet response rate that was half as high as the Dillman study and in which the postal mail got a significantly higher response rate than the e-mail strategy.

Both of these experiments were with populations that have virtually universal access to e-mail and used it routinely—and the survey request was identifiable as coming from an institution of which respondents were members. When survey requests come from less known or unknown sources and go to people who vary widely in how and how much they use the Internet, results are predictably variable. Sometimes, virtually no one responds.

The same kinds of steps that have been found to be helpful to postal surveys are likely to help enlist cooperative for Internet surveys: identifiable sponsors, well-designed instruments, financial incentives, and repeated contacts, including trying mail or phone requests for those who do not respond to an initial e-mail request. Dillman (2007) presents a thoughtful discussion of approaches to improving response rates.

Multimode Surveys

One of the best ways to minimize survey nonresponse is to use more than one mode to collect data. The key issues, as noted, are access, motivation, and cost. Mixing modes can enable researchers to reach people who are inaccessible via a single mode. It also can allow them to collect data from less intrinsically motivated sample members. For example, one attractive protocol is to use e-mail or mail for the first phase of data collection, followed by telephone interviews with nonrespondents. Combining telephone and in-person interviews is another effective design.

A critical issue in multimode surveys is the comparability of data across modes. Answers to some questions are affected by the mode of data collection; others are not. In order to combine data collected using different modes, it is important that the data are comparable. Those issues are discussed more in Chapter 5.

TWO OTHER APPROACHES TO
REDUCING NONRESPONSE ERROR

Proxy Respondents

Many surveys routinely collect data from one household respondent about other household members. If a respondent is unable or unwilling to be interviewed, asking another household member to report for the designated respondent is one option. Studies of the quality of such proxy data usually, but not always, indicate that proxy reporting is not as good as self-reporting for most topics. Moreover, few researchers would accept proxy reports of subjective states such as feelings, knowledge, or opinions. For factual information, however, if there is a knowledgeable proxy available, using proxy respondents can be an effective way to reduce error resulting from nonresponse. Groves (1989) reviews the inconclusive literature on the quality of data provided by proxy respondents.

Surveying Nonrespondents

Suppose a mail survey was done, and 60% of those sampled responded. The researcher thinks many nonrespondents would respond to a request to give a telephone or personal interview, but lacks the funds to try those procedures for all nonrespondents. An option is to draw a sample of nonrespondents to be contacted with the more expensive methods.

Two different uses can be made of such efforts.

First, the data from this second round of data collection can be used to estimate the direction and amount of bias in the initial sample. Of course, the second round also will have nonresponse, so it may produce data that do not fully represent all nonrespondents. However, subject to that limitation, the data may be used to improve the statistical adjustments (discussed in Chapter 10). With this perspective, the researcher might ask only a subset of the key questions, rather than all the questions, as one way of increasing the chances that a reluctant respondent might agree to cooperate. Some research organizations use significant financial incentives in these efforts as well.

Second, if the new round of data collection replicates questions in the initial survey, the results can be added to the initial sample data set. To do that, the data need to be weighted to adjust for the fact that only a sample of non-respondents received the follow-up treatment.

If half the nonrespondents are followed up, then the respondents from this phase of data collection should be weighted by a factor of two when they are combined with the initial data. Moreover, the results can be appropriately reported as reflecting an adjusted percentage of the sample population (an adjusted response rate), calculated as follows:

$$\text{Adjusted Response Rate} = \frac{\text{Phase I Responses} + 2 \times \text{Responses From Phase II}}{\text{Original Eligible Sample}}$$

NONPROBABILITY (OR MODIFIED PROBABILITY) SAMPLES

The discussion in this chapter so far has assumed a probability sample design whereby respondents are designated by some objective procedure. The researcher's problem is to collect data about those designated. However, as we have been discussing, often it is difficult and expensive to get responses from a high percentage of a probability sample, particularly a general population sample that on average has no particular reason to be invested in a particular survey. It is therefore understandable that investigators have explored alternative approaches to easing the data collection burden.

Substituting Respondents

The disagreement among survey researchers about the importance of probability sampling is intriguing. The federal government generally will not fund survey research efforts designed to make estimates of population characteristics that are not based on probability sampling techniques. Most academic survey organizations and many nonprofit research organizations have a similar approach to sampling. At the same time, almost all of the major public opinion polling groups, political polling groups, and market research organizations rely heavily on nonprobability sampling methods (see Converse, 1987, for a discussion of the historical roots of this difference).

The heart of probability sampling strategies is that the inclusion of someone in a sample is based on a predetermined procedure that sets a rate of selection for defined population subgroups. Beyond that, neither respondent characteristics nor interviewer discretion influence the likelihood that a person will be in a sample. Although nonprobability modifications of sampling procedures vary, they all share the property that, at the last stage, interviewer discretion and/or respondent characteristics not part of the sample design affect the likelihood of being included in a sample. The two most common procedures are described below.

For a personal interview study involving nonprobabilistic sampling, the researcher might draw blocks in much the same way that a sampler would draw blocks for an area probability sample. The difference would be that once a block was selected, the interviewer would be instructed to visit that block and complete some fixed number of interviews with people who reside on the block. There would be no specific listing of housing units on the block. One approach is to give the interviewer freedom to call on any home located on that block; the interviewer would not make callbacks to find people not at home on the initial visit.

A similar strategy is used for telephone surveys. Within a particular exchange, or cluster of numbers within an exchange, a target is set for completing a certain number of interviews. If there is no answer or no available respondent at the time the interviewer calls, another number is called from within the same cluster until the desired number of interviews is obtained. The first stage of sampling, if it is carried out as indicated above, distributes the sample around a geographic area more or less in the way that the population is distributed. At the point of household and respondent selection, however, there are three very clear kinds of biases that can be introduced.

In the personal interview strategy, but not the telephone strategy, interviewers can make a choice about which houses to visit. It turns out that interviewers will visit more attractive houses rather than less attractive houses, and first-floor apartments rather than second- and third-floor apartments. Interviewers also prefer housing units without dogs. Other factors that influence choices made by individual interviewers can be left to the reader's imagination.

Some research organizations attempt to restrict interviewer discretion by providing instructions about where on the block to start and asking interviewers not to skip housing units. Without an advance listing of units on the block, however, it is virtually impossible to evaluate whether or not an interviewer carried out those instructions. Moreover, if there is an advance listing of units on the street, one portion of the cost savings of this approach is eliminated.

In addition to the potential to substitute the households at which interviews are taken, there is great value in taking an interview with any household adult who is available and willing to be interviewed. Probability sampling requires specifying a respondent within a household by some objective method; in contrast, the substitution strategies permit interviews with any member of a contacted household who is willing to be interviewed.

One of the most obvious potentially biasing features of the nonprobability methods is the effect of availability. If one is not going to call back to the housing units where no one was home, or call back for household members who were not at home when the interviewer made contact, people who spend more time at home have a higher chance of being selected than those who routinely are not at home.

Uncontrolled sampling in this way produces some obvious sample biases. The most common approach to increasing the quality of the samples is to introduce quotas for obvious biases. Thus an interviewer may be required to interview half males and half females from any particular block or telephone cluster. Occasionally, some additional constraints will be set, such as the expected racial composition or the number of old or young adults. It is important, though, not to put too many constraints on the quotas, or interviewers will have to spend a great deal of time calling or wandering around blocks looking for eligible respondents.

The final bias inherent in allowing substitution has to do with the enlistment of cooperation. In the event that a respondent says he or she is busy or that it is not a good time to be interviewed, the interviewer has no incentive to enlist cooperation. If a project is not effectively presented, a significant fraction of the population will not be interested in helping. Letting people refuse easily without strenuous effort to present the study to them not only will bias a sample against the busy people, it also will bias it against the people who have less prior knowledge or less intrinsic interest in research and/or in the particular subject matter being studied.

Sudman (1967, 1976) argues that there is nonresponse in all surveys, even those in which every effort is made to contact nonrespondents. Once it has been learned that an individual will not cooperate or cannot be reached after several calls, he suggests that substituting a respondent from the same household or block actually may improve the quality of estimates. He argues that having a neighbor in the sample may be better than having neither the designated respondent nor his or her neighbor in the sample. When careful control is exercised over the interviewers' discretion, however, as Sudman advocates, the savings in reduced callbacks are offset largely by increased supervisory costs.

Nonprobability sampling methods produce cost savings for personal interview surveys (less so for telephone surveys). One other critical advantage of these methods, particularly for political surveys, is that they make it possible to conduct surveys overnight or in a few days. There are many people for whom many callbacks over several days are needed to catch them at home. Quick surveys obviously have to rely mainly on response from people who are more available.

When a quota sample is effectively implemented, the resulting samples often look rather similar to probability sample data, to the extent that they can be compared. Even so, two facts should be kept in mind. First, because the key to saving money is to make no callbacks, only about a third of the population has a chance to be in most nonprobability sample polls (i.e., the population that is at home on a typical first call). A sample that only gives a third of the population a chance to be selected, a third of the population with known distinctive characteristics, has great potential to be atypical in ways that will affect sample statistics.

Robinson (1989) provides an excellent example of how distorted a presumably well-done nonprobability sample can be. He compared results from two surveys, one based on a probability sample, the other on a nonprobability sample, both aimed at estimating interest in the arts and attendance at art-related events. The nonprobability sample survey greatly overestimated the level of interest in the arts.

In addition to potential bias, another downside of quota samples is that the assumptions of probability theory and sampling error, which routinely are touted as describing the reliability of nonprobability samples, do not apply. If there are substitutes, the sample is not a probability sample, though it may be spread around the population in a reasonably realistic way.

There are times when nonprobability samples are useful. Henry (1990) describes the various kinds of nonprobability samples and when they might be appropriate. If a researcher decides to use a nonprobability sample, however, readers should be told how the sample was drawn, the fact that it likely is biased in the direction of availability and willingness to be interviewed, and that the normal assumptions for calculating sampling errors do not apply. Such warnings to readers are not common. In many cases, nonprobability samples are misrepresented seriously, and that constitutes a serious problem for the credibility of social science research.

NONRESPONSE AS A SOURCE OF ERROR

Nonresponse is a problematic, important source of survey error. Table 4.2 demonstrates the great potential of nonresponse to effect results. Yet, although we can calculate a rate of response, we usually do not know the effect of nonresponse on data. The Keeter et al. (2006) study illustrates a survey with a comparatively low response rate producing results that are very similar to one with a much higher response rate, but the Groves (2006) analysis reminds us not to be complacent.

The key problem is that we usually lack good data about when nonresponse is and is not likely to be biased with respect to the content of the survey. Certainly one unintended positive effect of the increasing concerns about response rates is to increase pressure on researchers to collect data about non-response bias when they can. However, it is hard to do. In the absence of such data, perhaps the strongest argument for efforts to maximize response rates is credibility. When response rates are high, there is only a small potential for error due to nonresponse to be important. When response rates are low, there is great potential for important error; critics of the survey results have a reasonable basis on which to say the data are not credible.

EXERCISE

If a sample of housing units is selected as the first stage of sampling adults aged 18 or older, the response rate is the number of completed interviews divided by the number of individuals in the study population designated by the sampling procedure to be in the sample. Would you include or exclude the following groups from the denominator when calculating the response rate? (Why?)

Vacant housing units

Those who were away on vacation

Those temporarily in the hospital

Those who refused to be interviewed

Housing units in which all residents were under 18

Those who could not speak the researcher's language

Those who others in the households said were mentally ill or too confused to be interviewed

Those who were never at home when the interviewer called

Those who were away at college

Define the population to which your sample statistics (and your response rate) apply.

Further Readings

Dillman, D. A. (2007). *Mail and Internet surveys: The tailored design method* (2nd ed.). New York: John Wiley.

Groves, R. M., & Couper, M. P. (1998). *Nonresponse in household interview surveys.* New York: John Wiley.

Groves, R. M., Dillman, D. A., Eltinge, J. L., & Little, R. J. A. (Eds.). (2002). *Survey nonresponse.* New York: John Wiley.

5

Methods of Data Collection

The choice of data collection mode, mail, telephone, the Internet, personal interview, or group administration, is related directly to the sample frame, research topic, characteristics of the sample, and available staff and facilities; it has implications for response rates, question form, and survey costs. Computers can be used in the data collection process via all of these modes. An inventory of the various considerations in and consequences of the choice of a data collection mode is presented in this chapter.

One of the most far-reaching decisions a researcher must make is the way in which the data will be collected. Should an interviewer ask the questions and record the answers, or should the survey be self-administered? If an interviewer is to be used, there is the further decision about whether the interview will take place in person or over the telephone. If the respondent is to read and answer questions without an interviewer, there are choices about how to present the questionnaire to the respondents. In some cases, questionnaires are handed to respondents, in groups or individually, and returned immediately. In household surveys, questionnaires can be dropped off at a home or mailed and returned in a similar fashion. For those with Internet access, questions can be imbedded in e-mails or respondents can be asked to go to a Web site to answer questions.

Computers can be added to the mix in various ways. Of course, interviewers routinely use computers when doing telephone and in-person interviews. The more interesting variations have respondents entering answers directly into a computer. Surveys over the Internet involve no interviewer at all. Data can be collected in places where respondents go, such as doctors' offices, by having respondents answer questions into computers. Finally, over the telephone, a computerized voice can ask questions that are answered by using the touch-tone numbers.

Although the majority of surveys utilize a single data collection method, it is not uncommon for combinations of methods to be used. For example, personal interview surveys sometimes have series of questions that respondents answer by filling out a self-administered form or entering answers directly into a laptop computer. Computerized data collection has also been combined with telephone interviews. To reduce nonresponse, people who fail to return mail questionnaires sometimes are contacted by an interviewer on the phone or in person. Surveys using e-mail are often supplemented by mail survey protocols for those who lack an e-mail address or do not respond to e-mail. Respondents whom personal interviewers are unable to find at home or who have moved out of an area may be interviewed by telephone or asked to complete a self-administered form. Finally, some household surveys utilize telephone interviews for people at addresses for which telephone numbers can be obtained, but use a personal interviewer in households for which no telephone number can be found.

There are conditions under which each of these approaches to data collection is the best. In this chapter, the goal is to discuss the bases on which to choose among the various data collection approaches.

MAJOR ISSUES IN CHOOSING A STRATEGY

Sampling

The way a researcher plans to draw a sample is related to the best way to collect data. Certain kinds of sampling approaches make it easy or difficult to use one or another data collection strategy. If one is sampling from a list, the information on the list matters. Obviously, if a list lacks either good mailing addresses, good e-mail addresses, or good telephone numbers, trying to collect data by the corresponding mode is complicated. RDD greatly improved the potential of telephone data collection strategies by giving every household with a telephone a chance of being selected. Assuming one is willing to omit those without landline telephone service, it is perhaps the least expensive way to draw a general household sample.

Of course, it is possible to use random-digit-dialing strategies simply to sample and make initial contact with households, followed by data collection through the use of some other mode. Once a household has been reached, one can ask for a postal or e-mail address to permit an electronic or paper questionnaire to be sent or an interviewer to visit. Such designs are particularly useful when one is looking for a rare population, because both the sampling and the screening via telephone are comparatively less expensive than doing the same task with a personal interviewer. The difficulty with such strategies may lie in the rate of cooperation at the time of data collection.

When the basis of the sample is a set of addresses, either from a list or from an area probability sample, telephone, personal interview, and mail procedures all may be feasible. Obviously, if one has a good address, one can send an interviewer. In addition, it is possible to obtain telephone numbers for many addresses using commercial or Internet services that match names and addresses to published numbers and Directory Assistance.

Such approaches will not produce telephone numbers for all addresses. Therefore, some other mode of data collection will be needed as a supplement. It often is possible to interview a majority by telephone, however, thereby realizing the potential advantages of that mode. If one samples from a good list of addresses, a mail survey also is feasible. In an urban area with many multiunit dwellings, though, it is important that there be apartment unit designations (or household names) as well as a street address. Without an apartment unit or name, a mailing to a multiunit structure will go undelivered or will not reach the right unit. The problem is equally troublesome in rural areas where people may receive their mail in post office boxes. If a rural sample frame does not include names or addresses at people's houses, a mail survey is out of the question.

Sample listings that include e-mail addresses obviously open that avenue of data collection. While e-mail is not yet a reasonable option for general population surveys, there are many populations (employees, students, members of professional organizations) for which e-mail addresses are nearly universal and are easily available. In those cases, using the Internet as the main, or at least one, data collection mode may be a good idea.

A final sampling issue to consider is designating a respondent. If the sample frame is a list of individuals, any procedure, including mail, is feasible. Many surveys, however, entail designating a specific respondent at the time of data collection. If a questionnaire is mailed to a household or organization, the researcher has little control over who actually completes the questionnaire. Therefore, the involvement of an interviewer is a critical aid if respondent designation is an issue.

Type of Population

The computer skills of the population, their reading and writing skills, and their motivation to cooperate are salient considerations in choosing a mode of data collection. Self-administered approaches to data collection place more of a burden on the reading and writing skills of the respondent than do interviewer procedures, and computer use and skills are added if one is considering an Internet approach. Respondents who are not very well educated, whose reading and writing skills in English are less than facile (but who can speak English), people who do not see well, people who do not use computers very much, and people who are somewhat ill or tire easily all will find an interviewer-administered survey easier than filling out a self-administered form.

Another problem for self-administered approaches is getting people to return a completed questionnaire. If no interviewer is involved, the intrinsic motivation of the respondent is likely to be critical to who responds; people who are particularly interested in the research problem tend to be most likely to respond (Fowler et al., 2002; Heberlein & Baumgartner, 1978; Jobber, 1984). In this context, if one is collecting data from a population that is highly literate and that, on the average, is likely to be highly interested in the research, procedures such as mail or e-mail become more attractive. At the other extreme, if one is dealing with a population in which reading and writing skills are likely to be low and/or where the average level of interest and motivation is estimated to be low, interviewer-administered data collection strategies are likely to be preferable.

Ease of contact is another consideration. Interviewer-administered strategies depend on an interviewer being able to contact the respondent and make arrangements for data collection. One great advantage of the self-administered strategies is that if the contact information is correct, the questions will get to the respondents. Moreover, busy people can respond at any time that is convenient for them. On the other hand, if a survey is work related, busy people in work settings are used to talking on the telephone and to making appointments; they often have people who will schedule appointments for them. Making an appointment for a telephone interview can be the best way to collect data from such people.

Question Form

Generally speaking, if one is going to have a self-administered questionnaire, one must reconcile oneself to closed questions, that is, questions that can be answered by simply checking a box or circling the proper response from a set provided by the researcher. In part, that is because ease of response is a priority to maximize returns. Second, self-administered open answers often do not produce useful data. With no interviewer present to probe incomplete answers for clarity and for meeting consistent question objectives, the answers will not be comparable across respondents, and they will be difficult to code. If such answers are useful at all, it usually is when they are treated as anecdotal material, not as measures.

Although open-ended questions usually require an interviewer, there are also some instances when closed questions can be handled better by self-administered procedures. One very good example is when a researcher wants to ask a large number of items that are in a similar form. Having an interviewer read long lists of similar items can be awkward and tedious. On such occasions, a good strategy may be to put the questions in a self-administered form either in a questionnaire or on the computer. Such an approach also provides a welcome change of pace for an interview.

Self-administered procedures also have an advantage when question response categories are numerous or complex. In a personal interview, it is common to hand the respondent a card listing responses to help respondents keep all the possible answers in mind. Telephone surveys, however, require some adjustments. Three approaches are used. First, researchers simply may limit response scales for telephone interviews. Some have argued that four categories is a comfortable maximum on the telephone; for many telephone surveys, two- or three-category responses predominate.

Second, a longer list can be handled if a telephone interviewer reads the categories slowly, then reads them again, with the respondent choosing the correct category when the interviewer gets to it. It has not been demonstrated, however, that answers obtained in this way are identical to those given to a visual list of categories. For some kinds of questions, the answers are affected by the order in which responses are read (Bishop, Hippler, Schwarz, & Strack, 1988; Schuman & Presser, 1981).

Third, researchers can break down complex questions into a set of two or more simpler questions. For example, it is common to ask people to report their income in more than four or five categories. A nine-category question can be asked in two phases as follows: Would you say that your total family income is less than $30,000, between $30,000 and $60,000, or more than $60,000? Then, depending on the answer, the interviewer proceeds to ask another three-alternative question, such as: Well, would you say that your total family income was less than $40,000, $40,000 to $50,000, or more than $50,000? These variations do work to make questions answerable, but sometimes the question form itself affects the answers (Groves, 1989).

There are question forms, including those with complex descriptions of situations or events and those requiring pictures or other visual cues, that cannot be adapted to the telephone. If such measurement is a critical part of a survey, some form other than the telephone probably is needed. Researchers have shown, though, that they can adapt the majority of survey questions to telephone use. If an instrument is to be used in both interviewer and self-administered modes, it is wise to design the interview version first. It usually requires fewer changes to adapt an interview schedule to self-administration than vice versa.

Computer-based modes provide a number of advantages that cannot be replicated with paper and pencils. For example, rules for which questions to ask that are contingent on the answers to more than one question are nearly impossible to follow without computer assistance. Sometimes it is desirable to randomize the order of questions or response alternatives—an easy task with a computer, almost impossible without computer assistance.

Finally, when respondents are working directly with a computer, much more complicated material can be included in a survey. Thus, pictures, audio material, and combinations thereof can be presented to respondents as part of the survey process.

Question Content

Many studies have compared the results of different data collection strategies (e.g., Cannell et al., 1987; Groves & Kahn, 1979; Hochstim, 1967; Mangione, Hingson, & Barret, 1982). Good summaries of results are by de Leeuw and van der Zouwen (1988) and Dillman (2007). For most survey questions studied, the aggregate distributions obtained by personal interview, telephone interview, and self-administered procedures have been very similar.

Researchers have argued persuasively that one or another of the strategies should have an advantage when dealing with sensitive topics. Self-administered procedures are thought to be best because the respondent does not have to admit directly to an interviewer a socially undesirable or negatively valued characteristic or behavior. Others have argued that telephone procedures lend an air of impersonality to the interview process that should help people report negative events or behaviors. Moreover, random-digit dialing at least provides the option of having a virtually anonymous survey procedure, because the interviewer need not know the name or location of the respondent. Still others argue that personal interviewers are the best way to ask sensitive questions, because interviewers have an opportunity to build rapport and to establish the kind of trust that is needed for respondents to report potentially sensitive information.

Though all of these arguments sound plausible, the data clearly indicate that sensitive information is more frequently, and almost certainly more accurately, reported in self-administered modes than when interviewers ask the questions. Both self-administered paper forms and computer-assisted self-administration have been shown to produce the same results in comparison to interviewer administered protocols (Aquilino, 1994; Dillman & Tarnai, 1991; Tourangeau & Smith, 1998; Turner et al., 1998). Moreover, these results apply to very sensitive material (such as illegal drug use and sexual behavior) and more subtle issues related to self-image, such as reported health status or the prevalence of "problems" after prostate surgery (Fowler, Roman, & Di, 1998; McHorney, Kosinki, & Ware, 1994). If potentially sensitive answers are an important focus of a survey, finding a way to get those answers without interviewer involvement will almost certainly improve the estimates.

When comparing telephone and in-person interviews in this respect, the data are not as clear (de Leeuw & van der Zouwen, 1988). However, it is probably most common for a telephone procedure to show differences in the direction suggesting a social desirability bias in the answers, compared with personal interviews. One of the most striking such differences was found by Mangione and colleagues (1982) in the rate at which people admitted having past drinking problems. Hochstim (1967), Henson, Roth, and Cannell (1977), Aquilino (1994), and Fowler et al. (1998) found consistent results.

An entirely different aspect of question content that may affect the mode of data collection is the difficulty of the reporting task. In some surveys, researchers want to ask about events or behaviors that are difficult to report with accuracy because they extend over a period of time or are quite detailed. In such cases, reporting accuracy may benefit from a chance to consult records or to discuss the questions with other family members. The standard interview is a quick question-and-answer process that provides little such opportunity; this is especially true for telephone interviews. Self-administered procedures provide more time for thought, for checking records, and for consulting with other family members.

When great detail about small events is desired, such as information about what people eat or how they spend their money, or what television programs they watched, the very best approach is to have respondents keep a diary. Although there are limits to how many people will keep a diary, and often respondents are paid for doing so, it is a good way to get details. There are computerized alternatives to a paper diary, including having people periodically call an 800 number or give information over the Internet, that may be practical and can achieve the same data quality.

Overall, when samples are comparable, researchers have found that many survey estimates are unaffected by the mode of data collection. Unless some of the issues outlined above are very central to the research project, it is likely that the decision about how to collect data should be made on grounds other than the interaction between the subject matter of the questionnaire and the mode of data collection. Nonetheless, attention to the way question form or content might interact with mode of data collection to affect the results is an important part of the survey design process.

Response Rates

The rate of response is likely to be much more salient in the selection of a data collection procedure than other considerations. Obviously, one of the great strengths of group-administered surveys, when they are feasible, is the high rate of response. Generally speaking, when students in classrooms or workers at job settings are asked to complete questionnaires, the rate of response is near 100%. The limits on response usually stem from absenteeism or scheduling (shifts, days off).

The response rate for mail or e-mail surveys depends critically on the population and the survey's purpose. A survey of prostate surgery patients covered by Medicare achieved an 82% return by mail before telephone contacts brought the return rate over 90% (Fowler et al., 1998). In contrast, there are mail surveys done that achieve returns from fewer than 20% of those surveyed.

There is no doubt that the problem of nonresponse is central to the use of mail surveys. As noted in the previous chapter, if one simply mails questionnaires to a general population sample without appropriate follow-up procedures, the rate of return is likely to be less than 50% (Heberlein & Baumgartner, 1978). If extensive and appropriate follow-up procedures are utilized and if the project is otherwise well designed and executed, response rates often can be obtained for mail surveys that are similar to rates obtained using other modes (e.g., Dillman, 2007, Fowler et al., 1998).

The effectiveness of telephone strategies in producing high response rates depends in part on the sampling scheme. One way of utilizing the telephone for surveys is to replicate personal interview procedures. If one has a list of addresses as well as telephone numbers, an advance letter can be mailed introducing the study and explaining the purposes. After that, an interviewer can call on the telephone and ask for cooperation. Under these circumstances, telephone and personal response rates do not differ significantly. This is particularly true if interviewers can offer the option to nonrespondents of being interviewed in person (Groves, 1989; Hochstim, 1967; Mangione et al., 1982).

The procedures outlined above, however, are representative of only a minority of telephone surveys. Much more common are studies that link the telephone with random-digit-dialing sampling. One distinctive characteristic of RDD is that advance notice is not usually sent, though some organizations use reverse-address directories and send letters when an address is matched to a selected number. For a variety of reasons, response rates to random-digit-dialing telephone surveys have been falling over the past decade. That phenomenon, plus the rise of cell phone use, have made the representativeness of random-digit-dialing samples of increasing concern.

In conclusion, for list samples when advance letters are possible, and telephone coverage is nearly universal, there is little difference between telephone and personal interview procedures with respect to response. Moreover, when researchers want to reinterview people previously interviewed to get further information, the rate of response via the telephone is not different from that obtained by personal interviewers. For broader populations, it appears that one of the costs of random-digit-dialing telephone surveys is that the rate of response of selected households is lower, often much lower, than would be obtained by a personal interview survey. When a 5% to 20% reduction in response rates is multiplied by the rate at which people without phones, or landlines, also are omitted from such samples, the differential in the rate of response is not trivial. This is a disadvantage that researchers must be prepared to accept, or to work very hard to avoid, when they choose a random-digit-dialing approach.

Costs

The great appeal of mail and telephone survey procedures is that they usually cost less per return than personal interviews. Least expensive of all, of course, are surveys using the Internet. Survey costs depend on a multitude of factors. Some of the more salient factors are the amount of professional time required to design the questionnaire, time to program and test the computer-assisted program, the questionnaire length, the geographic dispersion of the sample, the availability and interest of the sample, the callback procedures, respondent selection rules, and the availability of trained staff.

The perceived costs for a mail survey can be misleading. The cost of postage, of clerical time for mailing, and of printing questionnaires turns out not to be trivial. Moreover, if there are telephone reminder calls, the expense gets higher.

Another key to the comparison is the telephone charges that are involved. Telephone use costs also will affect the personal-telephone cost comparison, but personal household interviews almost always will cost more per interview than telephone interviews with the same sample. Necessarily, the wages and expenses for an interviewer to visit a house and make contact with a respondent will exceed those for telephoning.

The comparative costs of mail and telephone modes will also depend on the population. If it is a highly motivated sample that readily returns surveys, mail costs will be lower than telephone costs. However, in a more typical case, to achieve similar rates of response, mail and phone modes may be fairly similar.

Although the choice between mail and telephone surveys often can be made on grounds unrelated to cost, cost usually has to play a role in choosing a personal interview procedure. Yet there are many cases in which the strengths of the personal interview procedure make it the best choice to achieve a given set of research objectives.

Finally, of course, if a survey can be done over the Internet, the costs per return potentially are the lowest of all. Depending on the kind of data collection, there may be some initial investment in software. Other than that, the main data collection cost is the staff time to design the survey instrument and test it. The key issues after the comparisons with other modes, of course, are whether or not an appropriate sample can be contacted via e-mail and the rate of response that can be achieved.

Available Facilities

The facilities and staff available should be considered in choosing a data collection mode. The development of an interviewing staff is costly and difficult. Attrition rates are generally high for newly trained interviewers. Many new interviewers are not very good at enlisting cooperation of respondents, producing high refusal rates at the start. In addition, people who are good at training and supervising interviewers are not easy to find. Thus one very practical consideration for anyone thinking about doing an interviewer-conducted survey is the ability to execute a professional data collection effort. If one has access to an ongoing survey operation or if staff members have experience in interviewer supervision and training, interviewer studies become more feasible. If not, self-administered surveys have a real advantage.

Length of Data Collection

The time involved in data collection varies by mode. Mail surveys usually take 2 months to complete. A normal sequence involves mailing the questionnaires, waiting for a while, doing some more mailing, some more waiting, and some eventual telephone or in-person follow-up. Of course, the Internet eliminates the time waiting for delivery, but it still usually involves repeated contacts and reminders. At the other extreme, it is quite feasible to do telephone surveys in a few days. The very quickest surveys pay a cost in nonresponse, because some people cannot be reached during any short period. Telephone surveys routinely, however, can be done more quickly than mail or personal household interview surveys of comparable size.

The length of time required to do a personal household interview survey defies generalization, simply because it depends so much on the sample size and the availability of staff. It is safe to say, though, that it is only a very unusual circumstance in which the data collection period for personal interviewing would not be greater than for a comparable telephone survey.

Computer-Assisted Data Collection

The traditional survey has relied on paper-and-pencil procedures, in the hands of either interviewers or respondents. In the past decade, however, computers have displaced paper and pencils: Questions to be asked pop up on a computer screen to be read by interviewers or respondents, and answers are recorded by keying codes into the computer. The principal advantage of computer-assisted data collection is having answers instantaneously in machine-readable form.

For some surveys, there also are advantages for data collection:

- The computer can follow complex question skip patterns that are difficult in a paper-and-pencil version.

- Information from previous questions, or even from previous interviews, can be taken into account in question wording or the sequence of questions asked.

- If inconsistent data are given, the computer can identify the inconsistency, and it can be reconciled at the point of data collection.

Offsetting these advantages, considerable lead time is needed to make sure the computer-assisted data collection is error free, and as is discussed in somewhat more detail in Chapter 9, researchers lose the ability to check or exercise any quality control over the data entry process. So, like most decisions about survey design, the value of having computer-assisted data collection varies with the requirements of each individual project. Couper and colleagues (1998) present the most recent studies related to computer-assisted data collection.

Computer assistance is used most commonly in connection with telephone surveys. In fact, to some people, computer-assisted telephone interviewing (CATI) is virtually synonymous with a telephone survey. To date, there is no documentation that the quality of data from telephone surveys is affected by whether or not data collection is computer assisted, except for reduction in missing data (Catlin & Ingram, 1988). Most of the documented advantages and disadvantages are practical: the ease of managing question form and order, the speed of data entry, sample management, and the potential to provide interviewers with "help" in the form of instructions or definitions as needed. The disadvantages include the need for error-free programs, the difficulty of interviewers going back to make corrections, and the risk of computer systems going down. In addition, although questions in narrative form can be handled by having interviewers type in verbatim answers, computer-assisted data collection further increases pressure to ask only fixed-response questions.

Most computer-assisted interviewing is done from a centralized telephone facility. With lightweight portable computers, however, personal household interviewers also carry out computer-assisted data collection. In addition, in selected settings, such as physicians' offices, computers have been used to collect data from people in a self-administered way: Respondents sit down at a computer, read questions on a screen, and respond by entering answers without benefit of an interviewer. Computers with touch screens or mouse capabilities are particularly suitable for such data collection efforts. The advantages of computer-assisted personal interviewing (CAPI) are about the same as those for CATI: ease of question management and rapid compilation of data. At the end of an interviewing day, an interviewer can transmit data to a central office over telephone lines.

Although computer assistance for self-administered surveys is still evolving, there are some additional interesting potentials that are likely to be realized. For example, computers make it possible to present information and stimuli in forms other than words (e.g., pictures).

Computers have the potential to adjust the language of the questions to the language of the respondent, as well as to read questions out loud for those who have difficulty reading. The ability of computers to alter the choice or sequence of questions to fit previous answers is a particular strength in self-administration, where complex skip instructions are difficult for respondents. Call-in computers can ask questions and record answers via touch-tone data entry, offering an alternative to the Internet to let respondents provide data at any time they choose. Finally, respondents appear to be more comfortable keying sensitive information into computers than providing the same information to an interviewer.

SUMMARY COMPARISON OF METHODS

The preceding discussion is not exhaustive, but it does cover most of the major considerations. The choice of a data collection mode is a complex one that involves many aspects of the survey research process. A summary of the strengths and weaknesses of the main approaches to collecting data follows.

Potential advantages of personal interviewing:

- Some sample designs can be implemented best by personal interview (e.g., area probability samples).
- Personal interview procedures are probably the most effective way of enlisting cooperation for most populations.
- Advantages of interviewer administration such as answering respondent questions, probing for adequate answers, accurately following complex instructions or sequences are realized.
- Multimethod data collection including observations, visual cues, and self-administered sections, on paper forms or into a computer, are feasible.
- Rapport and confidence building are possible (including any written reassurances that may be needed for reporting very sensitive material).
- Probably, longer survey instruments are possible in person than by any other mode.

Potential disadvantages of personal interviewing:

- It is likely to be more costly than the alternatives.
- A trained staff of interviewers that is geographically near the sample is needed.
- The total data collection period is likely to be longer than telephone procedures.
- Some samples (those in high-rise buildings or high-crime areas, elites, employees, students) may be more accessible by some other mode.

Potential advantages of telephone interviewing:

- Unit costs are usually lower than for personal interviews.
- Random-digit dialing (RDD) can be used to sample general populations.
- It provides better access to certain populations, especially compared to personal interviews.
- Data collection periods are usually shorter than for alternatives.
- The advantages of interviewer administration (in contrast with mail or Internet surveys) can be realized.
- Interviewer staffing and management is easier than for personal interviews: A smaller staff is needed, it is not necessary to be near the sample, and supervision and quality control potentially are better.
- There is likely to be a better response rate from a list sample than from a mail sample.

Potential disadvantages of telephone studies:

- There may be sampling limitations, especially as a result of omitting those without landline telephones or the inability to contact those on a list if a correct phone number cannot be found.
- Nonresponse associated with random-digit-dialing sampling is higher than for personal interviews.
- Questionnaire or measurement constraints are associated with the telephone, including limits on response alternatives, use of visual aids, and interviewer observations.
- Telephone is possibly less appropriate for personal or sensitive questions.

Potential advantages of self-administered (versus interviewer-administered) data collections:

- Presenting questions requiring visual aids is possible (in contrast to with telephone interviews).
- Asking questions with long or complex response categories is also feasible.

- Asking batteries of similar questions may be more acceptable to respondents.
- The fact that the respondent does not have to share answers with an interviewer makes collection of sensitive data likely more valid.

Potential disadvantages of self-administration:

- Especially careful questionnaire design is needed.
- Open questions usually are not useful.
- Good reading and writing skills are needed by respondents.
- The interviewer is not present to exercise quality control with respect to answering all questions, meeting question objectives, or the quality of answers provided.
- It is difficult to control who answers the questions.

Self-administered surveys can be done by mail, via group administration, or in households. Each approach has strengths and potential weaknesses.

Advantages of group administration:

- Cooperation rates are generally high.
- It provides a chance to explain the study and answer questions about questionnaire (in contrast to mail surveys).
- Generally, the unit costs are low.

The main disadvantage is that only a small number of surveys can use samples that can be gotten together in a group.

Advantages of mail procedures:

- Unit costs are relatively low.
- They can be accomplished with minimal staff and facilities.
- Mail provides access to widely dispersed samples and samples that for other reasons are difficult to reach by telephone or in person.
- Respondents have time to give thoughtful answers, to look up records, or to consult with others.

Disadvantages of mail procedures:

- Mail contact may not be an effective way to enlist cooperation (depending on the group to be studied and the topic).
- There are various disadvantages of not having interviewer involved in data collections.
- Good mailing addresses for the sample are needed.

Advantages of dropping off (and later picking up) questionnaires at households:

- The interviewer can explain the study, answer questions, and designate a household respondent, in contrast to mail.
- Response rates tend to be like those of personal interview studies.
- There is more opportunity for respondents to give thoughtful answers and consult records or other family members than in personal or telephone interview surveys.
- Trained interviewing staff is not required.

Disadvantages of dropping off questionnaires:

- This procedure costs about as much as personal interviews.
- A field staff is required (albeit perhaps a less thoroughly trained one than would be needed for personal interviews).

Potential advantages of Internet surveys:

- The unit cost of data collection is low.
- There is potential for high speed of returns.
- All the advantages of a self-administered instrument can be realized.
- All the advantages of a computer-assisted instrument can be realized.
- Like mail surveys, they provide time for thoughtful answers, checking records, or consulting with others.

Potential disadvantages of Internet surveys:

- Samples are limited to Internet users.
- Good addresses are needed.
- There is the challenge of enlisting cooperation (depending on the sampled groups and the topic).
- The various disadvantages of not having interviewer involved can affect the data collection.

Finally, when considering options, researchers also should consider combinations of modes. As noted, answers to many questions are not affected by mode of data collection. Combinations of personal, telephone, mail, and Internet procedures may offer the cost savings associated with the less expensive modes without the sampling or nonresponse prices they sometimes entail. Dillman (2007) and de Leeuw, Dillman, and Hox (2008) discuss some such combinations.

CONCLUSION

It is clear that the choice of mode is a complex decision and depends very much on the particular study situation. All of the above strategies are the best choice for some studies. It is appropriate, however, to note that the trend definitely has changed with respect to surveys of general, household-based samples. Thirty-five years ago, a researcher would have assumed that a personal interview survey was the method of choice for most studies. The burden of proof was on the person who would argue that another method could produce data that were as satisfactory.

Because of the cost advantages, in the last two decades of the 20th century, a researcher had to address directly the question of why an interviewer-administered survey could not be carried out by telephone. However, because of the widespread concerns about nonresponse to telephone surveys, the trend has changed again. While telephone surveys with random-digit-dialing samples are still widely done, there is a serious ongoing search for alternative ways to do general population surveys.

The role of self-administered techniques has grown in the past decade for two reasons. First, of course, the development of the Internet has opened a brand new approach to data collection. Researchers are eager to explore the Internet's potential. Second, considerable research evidence has demonstrated that self-administered procedures, particularly those that are computer assisted, can collect better data about sensitive topics than can interviewers. Those findings, along with expanding research into areas such as drug use and risky sexual behavior, have led to increased interest in integrating those strategies into data collection protocols.

Finally, it should be clear that the total survey design approach is critical when making a decision regarding mode of data collection. A smaller sample of personal interviews may produce a more useful data set than a larger sample of telephone interviews for the same price. A good sense of methodological goals and thoughtful consideration of all the design issues affecting cost and data quality are necessary before an appropriate decision can be made about how to collect survey data.

EXERCISE

Disregarding monetary costs, describe a survey research problem for which a mail survey would probably be the best choice, and explain why it would be better than the alternatives. Do the same for a random-digit telephone survey, for a personal interview household survey, and a survey using the Internet for data collection.

Further Readings

de Leeuw, E. D. (2008). Choosing the method of data collection. In E. D. de Leeuw, J. J. Hox, & D. A. Dillman (Eds.), *International handbook of survey methodology* (pp. 113–135). Mahwah, NJ: Lawrence Erlbaum.

Dillman, D. A. (2007). *Mail and Internet surveys: The tailored design method* (2nd ed.). New York: John Wiley.

Groves, R. M., Fowler, F. J., Couper, M. P., Lepkowski, J. M., Singer, E., & Tourangeau, R. (2004). *Survey methodology* (Chap. 5). New York: John Wiley.

6

Designing Questions to Be Good Measures

In surveys, answers are of interest not intrinsically but because of their relationship to something they are supposed to measure. Good questions are reliable (providing consistent measures in comparable situations) and valid (answers correspond to what they are intended to measure). This chapter discusses theory and practical approaches to designing questions to be reliable and valid measures.

Designing a question for a survey instrument is designing a measure, not a conversational inquiry. In general, an answer given to a survey question is of no intrinsic interest. The answer is valuable to the extent that it can be shown to have a predictable relationship to facts or subjective states that are of interest. Good questions maximize the relationship between the answers recorded and what the researcher is trying to measure.

In one sense, survey answers are simply responses evoked in an artificial situation contrived by the researcher. The critical issue in this chapter is what an answer to a survey question tells us about some reality in which we have an interest. Let us look at a few specific kinds of answers and their meanings:

1. A respondent tells us that he voted for Kerry rather than Bush for president in 2004. The reality in which we are interested is which lever, if any, he pulled in the voting booth. The answer given in the survey may differ from what happened in the voting booth for any number of reasons. The respondent may have pulled the wrong lever and, therefore, not know for whom he really voted. The respondent could have forgotten for whom he voted. The respondent also could have altered his answer intentionally for some reason.

2. A respondent tells us how many times he went to the doctor for medical care during the past year. Is this the same number that the researcher would have come up with had he followed the respondent around for 24 hours every day during the past year? Problems of recall, of defining what constitutes a visit to a doctor, and of willingness to report accurately may affect the correspondence between the number the respondent gives and the count the researcher would have arrived at independently.

3. When a respondent rates her public school system as "good" rather than "fair" or "poor," the researcher will want to interpret this answer as reflecting evaluations and perceptions of that school system. If the respondent rated only one school (rather than the whole school system), tilted the answer to please the interviewer, or understood the question differently from others, her answer may not reflect the feelings the researcher tried to measure.

Many surveys are analyzed and interpreted as if the researcher knows for certain what the answer means. Studies designed to evaluate the correspondence between respondents' answers and true values show that many respondents answer many questions very well. Even so, to assume perfect correspondence between the answers people give and some other reality is naive. When answers are good measures, it is usually the result of careful design. In the following sections, specific ways that researchers can improve the correspondence between respondents' answers and the true state of affairs are discussed.

One goal of a good measure is to increase question reliability. When two respondents are in the same situation, they should answer the question in the same way. To the extent that there is inconsistency across respondents, random error is introduced, and the measurement is less precise. The first part of this chapter deals with how to increase the reliability of questions.

There is also the issue of what a given answer means in relation to what a researcher is trying to measure: How well does the answer correspond? The later two sections of this chapter are devoted to validity, the correspondence between answers and true values and ways to improve that correspondence (Cronbach & Meehl, 1955).

INCREASING THE RELIABILITY OF ANSWERS

One step toward ensuring consistent measurement is that each respondent in a sample is asked the same set of questions. Answers to these questions are recorded. The researcher would like to be able to make the assumption that differences in answers stem from differences among respondents in what they have to say rather than from differences in the stimuli to which respondents were exposed. The question's wording is obviously a central part of the stimulus.

A survey data collection is an interaction between a researcher and a respondent. In a self-administered survey, on paper or via a computer, the researcher speaks directly to the respondent through a written questionnaire or words on a computer screen. In other surveys, an interviewer reads the researcher's words to the respondent. In either case, the survey instrument is the protocol for one side of the interaction. In order to provide a consistent data collection experience for all respondents, a good question has the following properties:

- The researcher's side of the question-and-answer process is entirely scripted so that the questions as written fully prepare a respondent to answer questions.
- The question means the same thing to every respondent.
- The kinds of answers that constitute an appropriate response to the question are communicated consistently to all respondents.

Avoiding Inadequate Wording

The simplest example of inadequate question wording is when, somehow, the researcher's words do not constitute a complete question.

INCOMPLETE WORDING

	Bad	*Better*
6.1	Age?	What was your age on your last birthday?
6.2	Reason last saw doctor?	What was the medical problem or reason for which you most recently went to a doctor?

Interviewers (or respondents) will have to add words or change words in order to make answerable questions from the words in the left column. If the goal is to have all respondents answering the same questions, then it is best if the researcher writes the questions fully.

Sometimes optional wording is required to fit differing respondent circumstances. That does not mean, however, that the researcher has to give up writing the questions. If the interview is computer assisted, often the computer can tailor the question wording. If a paper interview schedule is used, a common convention is to put optional wording in parentheses. These words will be used by the interviewer when they are appropriate to the situation and omitted when they are not needed.

EXAMPLES OF OPTIONAL WORDING

6.3 Were you (or was anyone living here with you) attacked or beaten up by a stranger during the past year?

6.4 Did (you/he/she) report the attack to the police?

6.5 How old was (EACH PERSON) on (your/his/her) last birthday?

In example 6.3, the parenthetical phrase would be omitted if the interviewer already knew that the respondent lived alone. If more than one person lived in the household, though, the interviewer would include it. The parenthetical choice offered in 6.4 may seem minor. The parentheses, however, alert the interviewer to the fact that a wording choice must be made; the proper pronoun is used, and the principle is maintained that the interviewer need read only the questions exactly as written in order to present a satisfactory stimulus.

A variation that accomplishes the same thing is illustrated in 6.5. A format such as this might be used if the same question were to be used for each person in a household. Rather than repeat the identical words endlessly, a single question is written instructing the interviewer to substitute an appropriate designation (your husband/your son/your oldest daughter).

Whether on paper or via computer, the goal is to have the interviewer ask questions that make sense and take advantage of knowledge previously gained in the interview to tailor the questions to the respondent's individual circumstances. There is another kind of optional wording that is seen occasionally in questionnaires that is not acceptable.

EXAMPLE OF UNACCEPTABLE OPTIONAL WORDING

6.6   What do you like best about this neighborhood? (We're interested in anything, like houses, the people, the parks, or whatever.)

Presumably, this parenthetical probe was thought to be helpful to respondents who had difficulty in answering the question. From a measurement point of view, however, it undermines the principle of standardized interviewing. If interviewers use the parenthetical probe when a respondent does not readily come up with an answer, that subset of respondents will have answered a different question. Such optional probes usually are introduced when the researcher does not think the initial question is a very good one. The proper approach is to write a good question in the first place. Interviewers should not be given any options about what questions to read or how to read them except, as in the examples above, to make the questions fit the circumstances of a particular respondent in a standardized way.

The following is a different example of incomplete question wording. There are three errors embedded in the example.

EXAMPLE OF POOR WORDING

6.7   I would like you to rate different features of your neighborhood as very good, good, fair, or poor. Please think carefully about each item as I read it.

        a. Public schools

        b. Parks

    c. Public transportation

    d. Other

The first problem with 6.7 is the order of the main stem. The response alternatives are read prior to an instruction to think carefully about the specific items. The respondent probably will forget the question. The interviewer likely will have to do some explaining or rewording before a respondent will be prepared to give an answer. Second, the words the interviewer needs to ask about the items on the list are not provided. A much better question would be the following:

6.7a   I am going to ask you to rate different features of your neighborhood. I want you to think carefully about your answers. How would you rate (FEATURE)— would you say very good, good, fair, or poor?

The interviewer would sequentially insert each item (public schools, parks, etc.) until all four questions had been asked. This format gives the interviewer the wording needed for asking the first and all subsequent items on the list as complete questions. It also puts the elements of the question in the proper order, so that the response alternatives are read to the respondent at a point they are more likely to be remembered.

The third problem with the example is the fourth alternative, "other." What is the interviewer to say? Is he or she to make up some new question such as, "Is there anything else about your neighborhood you value?" How is the rating question to be worded? It is not uncommon to see "other" on a list of questions in a form similar to the example. Clearly, in the form presented in 6.7, the script is inadequate.

The above examples illustrate questions that could not be presented consistently to all respondents as a result of incomplete wording. Another step needed to increase consistency is to create a set of questions that flows smoothly and easily. If questions have awkward or confusing wording, if there are words that are difficult to pronounce, or if combinations of words sound awkward together, interviewers will change the words to make the questions sound better or to make them easier to read. It may be possible to train and supervise interviewers to keep such changes to a minimum. Nevertheless, it only makes sense to help interviewers by giving them questions that are as easy to read as possible.

Ensuring Consistent Meaning for All Respondents

If all respondents are asked exactly the same questions, one step has been taken to ensure that differences in answers can be attributed to differences in respondents. But there is a further consideration: The questions should all mean the same thing to all respondents. If two respondents understand the question to mean different things, their answers may be different for that reason alone. One potential problem is using words that are not understood universally. In general population samples, it is important to remember that a range of educational experiences and cultural backgrounds will be represented. Even with well-educated respondents, using simple words that are short and understood widely is a sound approach to questionnaire design.

Undoubtedly, a much more common error than using unfamiliar words is the use of terms or concepts that can have multiple meanings. The prevalence of misunderstanding of common wording has been well documented by those who have studied the problem (e.g., Belson, 1981; Fowler, 1992; Oksenberg, Cannell, & Kalton, 1991; Tanur, 1991; Tourangeau, Rips, & Rasinski, 2000).

POORLY DEFINED TERMS

6.8   How many times in the past year have you seen or talked with a doctor about your health?

Problem. There are two ambiguous terms or concepts in this question. First, there is basis for uncertainty about what constitutes a doctor. Are only people practicing medicine with M.D. degrees included? If so, then psychiatrists are included, but psychologists, chiropractors, osteopaths, and podiatrists are not. What about physicians' assistants or nurses who work directly for doctors in doctors' offices? If a person goes to a doctor's office for an inoculation that is given by a nurse, does this count?

Second, what constitutes seeing or talking with a doctor? Do telephone consultations count? Do visits to a doctor's office when the doctor is not seen count?

Solutions. Often the best approach is to provide respondents and interviewers with the definitions they need.

6.8a   We are going to ask about visits to doctors and getting medical advice from doctors. In this case, we are interested in all professional personnel who have M.D. degrees or work directly for an M.D. in the office, such as a nurse or medical assistant.

When the definition of what is wanted is extremely complicated and would take a very long time to define, as may be the case in this question, an additional constructive approach may be to ask supplementary questions about desired events that are particularly likely to be omitted. For example, visits to psychiatrists, visits for inoculations, and telephone consultations often are underreported and may warrant special follow-up questions. Asking specific follow-up questions to make sure such events were not left out is an easy way to reduce such errors.

POORLY DEFINED TERMS

6.9   Did you eat breakfast yesterday?

Problem. The difficulty is that the definition of breakfast varies widely. Some people consider coffee and a donut anytime before noon to be breakfast. Others do not consider that they have had breakfast unless it includes a major entree, such as bacon and eggs, and is consumed before 8 a.m. If the objective is to measure morning food consumption, the results are likely to contain considerable error stemming from differing definitions of breakfast.

Solutions. There are two approaches to the solution. On the one hand, one might choose to define breakfast:

6.9a   For our purposes, let us consider breakfast to be a meal, eaten before 10:00 in the morning, that includes some protein such as eggs, meat, or milk, some grain such as toast or cereal, and some fruit or vegetable, including juice. Using that definition, did you have breakfast yesterday?

Although this often is a very good approach, in this case it is very complicated. Instead of trying to communicate a common definition to respondents, the researcher may simply ask people to report what they consumed before 10 a.m. At the coding stage, what was eaten can be evaluated consistently to see if it meets the standards for breakfast, without requiring each respondent to share the same definition.

POORLY DEFINED TERMS

6.10   Do you favor or oppose gun control legislation?

Problem. Gun control legislation can mean banning the legal sale of certain kinds of guns, asking people to register their guns, limiting the number or the kinds of guns that people may possess, or limiting which people may possess them. Answers cannot be interpreted without assumptions about what respondents think the question means. Respondents will undoubtedly interpret this question differently.

6.10a   One proposal for the control of guns is that no person who ever had been convicted of a violent crime would be allowed to purchase or own a pistol, rifle, or shotgun. Would you oppose or support legislation like that?

One could argue that this is only one of a variety of proposals for gun control. That is exactly the point. If one wants to ask multiple questions about different possible strategies for gun control, one should ask separate specific questions that can be understood commonly by all respondents and interpreted by researchers. One does not solve the problem of a complex issue by leaving it to the respondents to decide what question they want to answer.

There is a potential tension between providing a complicated definition to all respondents and trying to keep questions clear and simple. This is particularly true for interviewer-administered surveys, as long definitions are particularly hard to grasp when they are delivered orally.

A potential approach is to tell interviewers to provide definitions to respondents who ask for clarification or appear to misunderstand a question. One concern about such approaches is that interviewers will not give consistent definitions if they have to improvise. However, computer-assisted interviewing makes it easy to provide interviewers with a precisely worded definition. The other, more important, concern is that only some respondents will get the needed definition. Those respondents who do not ask for clarification or appear confused will lack important information that might affect their answers.

Conrad and Schober (2000) experimented with giving interviewers freedom to provide definitions and explanations when they seemed needed. There was some evidence that accuracy improved, but the increases came at a price of more interviewer training and longer interviews. While there is need for more research on how to ask questions about complex concepts, the general approach of avoiding complex or ambiguous terms, and defining those that are used in the question wording, is the best approach for most surveys.

AVOIDING MULTIPLE QUESTIONS

Another way to make questions unreliable is to ask two questions at once.

6.11   Do you want to be rich and famous?

The problem is obvious: rich and famous are not the same. A person could want to be one but not the other. Respondents, when faced with two questions, will have to decide which to answer, and that decision will be made inconsistently by different respondents.

Most multiple questions are somewhat subtler, however.

6.12   In the last 30 days, when you withdrew cash from an ATM, how often did you withdraw less than $25—always, usually, sometimes, never?

This question requires three cognitive calculations: calculate the number of visits to an ATM, the number of times less than $25 was withdrawn, and the relationship between the two numbers. While technically there is only one question, it is necessary to answer at least two prior questions in order to produce the answer. It would be better question design to use two questions.

6.12a   In the last 30 days, how many times did you withdraw cash from an ATM?

6.12b   (IF ANY) On how many of those times did you withdraw less than $25?

Note two other virtues of the 6.12a and 6.12b series. First, it identifies those who did not use an ATM at all, to whom the question does not apply. Second, by asking for numbers in both questions, it avoids having respondents do a calculation. Simplifying the demands on respondents is almost always a good idea.

6.13   To what kind of place do you go for your routine medical care?

This question assumes that all respondents get routine medical care, which is not an accurate assumption. It should be asked as two questions. Probably the best approach is to ask if the respondent has gotten any routine medical care in some period—for example, the past 12 months. If so, follow with a question about the kind of place.

The "Don't Know" Option

When respondents are being asked questions about their own lives, feelings, or experiences, a "don't know" response is often a statement that they are unwilling to do the work required to give an answer. On the other hand, sometimes we ask respondents questions concerning things about which they legitimately do not know. As the subject of the questions gets further from their immediate lives, it is more plausible and reasonable that some respondents will not have adequate knowledge on which to base an answer or will not have formed an opinion or feeling. In those cases, we have another example of a question that actually is two questions at once: do you have the information needed to answer the question and, if so, what is the answer?

There are two approaches to dealing with such a possibility. One simply can ask the questions of all respondents, relying on the respondent to volunteer a "don't know" answer. Respondents differ in their willingness to volunteer that they "don't know," however (Schuman & Presser, 1981), and interviewers are inconsistent in how they handle "don't know" responses (Fowler & Mangione, 1990; Groves, 1989). The alternative is to ask all respondents a standardized screening question about whether or not they feel familiar enough with a topic to have an opinion or feeling about it.

When a researcher is dealing with a topic about which familiarity is high, whether or not a screening question for knowledge is asked is probably not important. When a notable number of respondents will not be familiar with, or have not thought about, whatever the question is dealing with, it probably is best to ask a screening question about familiarity with the topic.

Specialized Wording for Special Subgroups

Researchers have wrestled with the fact that the vocabularies in different subgroups of the population are not the same. One could argue that standardized measurement actually would require different questions for different subgroups (Schaeffer, 1992). Designing different forms of questionnaires for different subgroups, however, is almost never done. Rather, methodologists tend to work very hard to attempt to find wording for questions that has consistent meaning across an entire population. Even though there are situations where a question wording is more typical of the speech of one segment of a community than another (most often the better-educated segment), finding exactly comparable words for some other group of the population and then giving interviewers reliable rules for deciding when to ask which version is so difficult that it is likely to produce more unreliability than it eliminates.

The extreme challenge is how to collect comparable data from people who speak different languages. The most careful efforts translate an original version into the new language, have a different translator back translate the new version into the original language, and then try to reconcile the differences between the original and the back-translated version.

This process would be greatly improved if the designers of the original questions were concerned about ease of translation. For example, numbers translate more readily across languages than adjectives. Abstract concepts and words that are colloquial are likely to be particularly hard to translate accurately. Even when great care is taken, it is very hard to be sure people are answering comparable questions across languages. It is doubtful that adjectival rating scales are ever comparable across languages. The more concrete the questions, the better the chances for comparability of results across languages or cultures. Marin and Marin (1991) present a good analysis of the challenges of collecting comparable data from English and Spanish-speaking people. Harkness, Van de Vijver, and Mohler (2003) provide a comprehensive look at the challenges of collecting comparable data across cultures.

Standardized Expectations for Type of Response

As stated, it is important to give interviewers a good script so that they can read the questions exactly as worded, and it is important to design questions that mean the same thing to all respondents. The other key component of a good question is that respondents should have the same perception of what constitutes an adequate answer for the question.

The simplest way to give respondents the same perceptions of what constitutes an adequate answer is to provide them with a list of acceptable answers. Such questions are called closed questions. The respondent has to choose one, or sometimes more than one, of a set of alternatives provided by the researcher.

6.14   What was the main reason you went to the doctor—for a new health problem, for a follow-up for a previous health problem, for a routine checkup, or for some other reason?

Closed questions are not suitable in all instances. The range of possible answers may be more extensive than it is reasonable to provide. The researcher may not feel that all reasonable answers can be anticipated. For such reasons, the researcher may prefer not to provide a list of alternatives to the respondent. In that case, the question must communicate the kind of response wanted as well as possible.

6.15   When did you have the measles?

Problem. The question does not specify the terms in which the respondent is to answer. Consider the following possible answers: "Five years ago"; "While I was in the army"; "When I was pregnant with our first child"; "When I was 32"; "In 1987." All of these answers could be given by the same person, and all are appropriate answers to the question as posed. They are not all acceptable in the same survey, however, because descriptive statistics require comparable answers. An interviewer cannot use the words in example 6.14 and consistently obtain comparable data, because each respondent must guess what kind of answer is wanted.

Solution. A new question must be created that explains to the respondent what kind of answer is wanted.

6.15a   How old were you when you had the measles?

Obviously, 6.15a is the way the question should have been worded by the researcher for all respondents.

6.16   Why did you vote for candidate A?

Problems. Almost all "why" questions pose problems. The reason is that one's sense of causality or frame of reference can influence answers. In the particular instance above, the respondent may choose to talk about the strengths of candidate A, the weaknesses of candidate B, or the reasons he or she used

certain criteria (My mother was a lifelong Republican). Hence respondents
who see things exactly the same way may answer differently.

Solution. Specify the focus of the answer:

6.16a   What characteristics of candidate A led you to vote for (him/her) over candidate B?

Such a question explains to respondents that the researcher wants them to
talk about candidate A, the person for whom they voted. If all respondents
answer with that same frame of reference, the researcher then will be able to
compare responses from different respondents in a direct fashion.

6.17   What are some of the things about this neighborhood that you like best?

Problems. In response to a question like this, some people will only make one
or two points, whereas others will make many. It is possible that such differences reflect important differences in respondent perceptions or feelings.
Research has shown pretty clearly, however, that education is related highly to
the number of answers people give to such questions. Interviewers also affect
the number of answers.

Solution. Specify the number of points to be made:

6.17a   What is the feature of this neighborhood that you would single out as the one
you like most?

6.17b   Tell me the three things about this neighborhood that you like most about living here.

Although this may not be a satisfactory solution for all questions, for many
such questions it is an effective way of reducing unwanted variation in answers
across respondents.

The basic point is that answers can vary because respondents have a different understanding of the kind of responses that are appropriate. Better specifi-
cation of the properties of the answer desired can remove a needless source of
unreliability in the measurement process.

TYPES OF MEASURES/TYPES OF QUESTIONS

The above procedures are designed to maximize reliability, the extent to which
people in comparable situations will answer questions in similar ways. One
can measure with perfect reliability, though, and still not be measuring what

one wants to measure. The extent to which the answer given is a true measure and means what the researcher wants or expects it to mean is called *validity*. In this section, aspects of the design of questions are discussed, in addition to steps to maximize the reliability of questions, that can increase the validity of survey measures.

For this discussion, it is necessary to distinguish between questions designed to measure facts or objectively measurable events and questions designed to measure subjective states such as attitudes, opinions, and feelings. Even though there are questions that fall in a murky area on the border between these two categories, the idea of validity is somewhat different for objective and subjective measures.

If it is possible to check the accuracy of an answer by some independent observation, then the measure of validity becomes the similarity of the survey report to the value of some "true" measure. In theory, one could obtain an independent, accurate count of the number of times that an individual used an ATM during a year. Although in practice it may be very difficult to obtain such an independent measure (e.g., getting access to the relevant records could be impossible), the understanding of validity can be consistent for objective situations.

In contrast, when people are asked about subjective states, feelings, attitudes, and opinions, there is no objective way of validating the answers. Only the respondent has access to his or her feelings and opinions. Thus the validity of reports of subjective states can be assessed only by their correlations with other answers that a person gives or with other facts about the respondent's life that one thinks should be related to what is being measured. For such measures, there is no truly independent direct measure possible; the meaning of answers must be inferred from patterns of association.

Levels of Measurement

There are four different ways in which measurement is carried out in social sciences. This produces four different kinds of tasks for respondents and four different kinds of data for analysis:

Nominal—people or events are sorted into unordered categories (Are you male or female?)

Ordinal—people or events are ordered or placed in ordered categories along a single dimension (How would you rate your health—very good, good, fair, or poor?)

Interval data—numbers are attached that provide meaningful information about the distance between ordered stimuli or classes (in fact, interval data are very rare; Fahrenheit temperature is one of the few common examples)

Ratio data—numbers are assigned such that ratios between values are meaningful, as well as the intervals between them. Common examples are counts or measurements by an objective, physical scale such as distance, weight, or pressure (How old were you on your last birthday?)

Most often in surveys, when one is collecting factual data, respondents are asked to fit themselves or their experiences into a category, creating nominal data, or they are asked for a number, most often ratio data. "Are you employed?"; "Are you married?"; and "Do you have arthritis?" are examples of questions that provide nominal data. "How many times have you seen a doctor?"; "How much do you weigh?"; and "What is the hourly rate you are paid?" are examples of questions that ask respondents to provide real numbers for ratio data.

When gathering factual data, respondents may be asked for ordinal answers. For example, they may be asked to report their incomes in relatively large categories or to describe their behavior in nonnumerical terms (e.g., usually, sometimes, seldom, or never). When respondents are asked to report factual events in ordinal terms, it is because great precision is not required by the researcher or because the task of reporting an exact number is considered too difficult. There usually is a real numerical basis, however, underlying an ordinal answer to a factual question.

The situation is somewhat different with respect to reports of subjective data. Although there have been efforts over the years, first in the work of psychophysical psychologists (e.g., Thurstone & Chave, 1929), to have people assign numbers to subjective states that met the assumptions of interval and ratio data, for the most part respondents are asked to provide nominal and ordinal data about subjective states. The nominal question is, "Into which category do your feelings, opinions, or perceptions fall?" The ordinal question is "Where along this continuum do your feelings, opinions, or perceptions fall?"

When designing a survey instrument, a basic task of the researcher is to decide what kind of measurement is desired. When that decision is made, there are some clear implications for the form in which the question will be asked.

Types of Questions

Survey questions can be classified roughly into two groups: those for which a list of acceptable responses is provided to the respondent (closed questions) and those for which the acceptable responses are not provided exactly to the respondent (open questions).

When the goal is to put people in unordered categories (nominal data), the researcher has a choice about whether to ask an open or closed question. Virtually identical questions can be designed in either form.

EXAMPLES OF OPEN AND CLOSED QUESTIONS

6.18   What health conditions do you have? (open)

6.18a   Which of the following conditions do you currently have? (READ LIST) (closed)

6.19   What do you consider to be the most important problem facing our country today? (open)

6.19a   Here is a list of problems that many people in the country are concerned about. Which do you consider to be the most important problem facing our country today? (closed)

There are advantages to open questions. They permit the researcher to obtain answers that were unanticipated. They also may describe more closely the real views of the respondents. Third, and this is not a trivial point, respondents like the opportunity to answer some questions in their own words. To answer only by choosing a provided response and never to have an opportunity to say what is on one's mind can be a frustrating experience. Finally, open questions are appropriate when the list of possible answers is longer than is feasible to present to respondents.

Despite all this, however, closed questions are usually a more satisfactory way of creating data. There are four reasons for this:

1. The respondent can perform more reliably the task of answering the question when response alternatives are given.

2. The researcher can perform more reliably the task of interpreting the meaning of answers when the alternatives are given to the respondent (Schuman & Presser, 1981).

3. When a completely open question is asked, many people give relatively rare answers that are not analytically useful. Providing respondents with a constrained number of answer options increases the likelihood that there will be enough people giving any particular answer to be analytically interesting.

4. Since most data collection now is computer assisted, it is much easier for interviewers or respondents to record answers by checking a provided answer than to key in narrative answers.

Finally, if the researcher wants ordinal data, the categories must be provided to the respondent. One cannot order responses reliably along a single continuum unless a set of permissible ordered answers is specified in the question. Further discussion about the task that is given to respondents when they are asked to perform an ordinal task is appropriate, because it is probably the most prevalent kind of measurement in survey research.

FEELING ABOUT SOMETHING

Extremely Positive									Extremely Negative

TWO-CATEGORY SCALE

Good									Not Good

THREE-CATEGORY SCALE

Good				Fair					Poor

FOUR-CATEGORY SCALE

Very Good		Good			Fair				Poor

FIVE-CATEGORY SCALE

Excellent		Very Good		Good		Fair			Poor

ELEVEN-CATEGORY SCALE

10	9	8	7	6	5	4	3	2	1	0

Figure 6.1   Subjective Continuum Scales

Figure 6.1 shows a continuum. (This case concerns having respondents make a rating of some sort, but the general approach applies to all ordinal questions.) There is a dimension assumed by the researcher that goes from the most negative feelings possible to the most positive feelings possible. The way survey researchers get respondents into ordered categories is to put designations or labels on such a continuum. Respondents then are asked to consider the labels, consider their own feelings or opinions, and place themselves in the proper category.

There are two points worth making about the kinds of data that result from such questions. First, respondents will differ in their understanding of what the labels or categories mean. The only assumption that is necessary in order to make meaningful analyses, however, is that, on the average, the people who rate their feelings as "good" feel more positively than those who rate their feelings as "fair." To the extent that people differ some in their understanding of and criteria for "good" and "fair," there is unreliability in the measurement, but the measurement still may have meaning (i.e., correlate with the underlying feeling state that the researcher wants to measure).

Second, an ordinal scale measurement like this is relative. The distribution of people choosing a particular label or category depends on the particular scale that is presented.

Consider the rating scale in Figure 6.1 again and consider two approaches to creating ordinal scales. In one case, the researcher used a 3-point scale: good, fair, or poor. In the second case, the researcher used five descriptive options: excellent, very good, good, fair, and poor. When one compares the two scales, one can see that adding "excellent" and "very good" in all probability does not simply break up the "good" category into three pieces. Rather, it changes the whole sense of the scale. People respond to the ordinal position of categories as well as to the descriptors.

A recent experiment makes the point (Wilson, Alman, Whitaker, & Callegro, 2004). Respondents were asked to use two 5-point scales to rate their health—one identical to the 5-point scale in Figure 6.1 and the other using "very good, good, moderate, bad, and very bad." Respondents then were asked to use a scale from 1 to 10 to provide a numerical equivalent for each verbal category in the two scales.

As one would expect, the numbers given to "very good" were higher when it was the first answer (9.8 vs. 7.8) and "good" received a numerical score of 7.3 when it was the second category, but only 5.4 when it was third.

Such scales are meaningful if used as they are supposed to be used: to order people. By itself, however, a statement that some percentage of the population feels something is "good or better" is not appropriate, because it implies that the population is being described in some absolute sense. In fact, the percentage would change if the question were different. Only comparative statements (or statements about relationships) are justifiable when one is using ordinal measures:

- comparing answers to the same question across groups (e.g., 20% more of those in group A than in group B rated the candidate as "good or better"); or

- comparing answers from comparable samples over time (e.g., 10% more rated the candidate "good" or better in January than did so in November).

The same general comments apply to data obtained by having respondents order items (e.g., Consider the schools, police services, and trash collection. Which is the most important city service to you?). The percentage giving any item top ranking, or the average ranking of an item, is completely dependent on the particular list provided. Comparisons between distributions when the alternatives have been changed at all are not meaningful.

Agree-Disagree Items: A Special Case

Agree-disagree items are very prevalent in survey research and therefore deserve special attention. The task that respondents are given in such items is different from that of placing themselves in an ordered category. The usual approach is to read a statement to respondents and to ask them if they agree or disagree with that statement. The statement is located somewhere on a continuum such as that portrayed in Figure 6.1. Respondents' locations on that continuum are calculated by figuring out whether they say their feelings are very close to that statement (by agreeing) or are very far from where that statement is located (by disagreeing).

When one compares questions posed in the agree-disagree format with questions in the straightforward rating format, there are numerous disadvantages to the former. Compare the following:

6.20   My health is poor. Do you strongly agree, agree, disagree, or strongly disagree?

6.20a   How would you rate your health—excellent, very good, good, fair, or poor?

The disadvantages to the first statement are as follows:

• The rating scale sorts respondents into five categories; the agree-disagree question is almost always analyzed by putting respondents into two groups (agrees or disagrees). Hence more information is gained from the rating.

• Agree-disagree questions, in order to be interpretable, can only be asked about extremes of a continuum. If the statement was, "My health is fair," a person could disagree either because it was "good" or because it was "poor." This feature limits the ability to order people in the middle of a continuum.

• Respondents often find it confusing that the way to say their health is good is to disagree that their health is poor.

• Studies show that some respondents are particularly likely to agree (or acquiesce) when questions are put in this form; that is, there are people who would agree both that their health is "poor" and that it is "not poor" if question 6.20 was stated in the negative (Dillman & Tarnai, 1991; Krosnick, Judd, & Wittenbrink, 2007; Schuman & Presser, 1981).

Because of these complexities, it is routinely found that the direct rating task has more validity than the comparable agree-disagree question. For unidimensional scaling tasks, it is hard to justify using 6.20 rather than 6.20a. A very common usage of the format, however, is to obtain responses to complex statements such as the following:

6.21   With economic conditions the way they are these days, it really isn't fair to have more than two children.

This question is asking about at least three things at once: the perceived state of the economy, views on the appropriate maximum number of children, and views about the relationship between the economy and family size.

If a person does not happen to think that economic conditions are bad (which the question imposes as an assumption) and/or that economic conditions of whatever kind have any implications for family size, but if that person happens to think two children is a good target for a family, it is not easy to answer the question. Moreover, whether a person agrees or disagrees, it is hard to know what the respondent agreed or disagreed with.

The agree-disagree format appears to be a rather simple way to construct questions. In fact, to use this form to provide reliable, useful measures is not easy and requires a great deal of care and attention. Usually, researchers will have more reliable, valid, and interpretable data if they avoid the agree-disagree question form.

INCREASING THE VALIDITY
OF FACTUAL REPORTING

When a researcher asks a factual question of a respondent, the goal is to have the respondent report with perfect accuracy; that is, give the same answer that the researcher would have given if the researcher had access to the information needed to answer the question. There is a rich methodological literature on the reporting of factual material. Reporting has been compared against records in a variety of areas, in particular the reporting of economic and health events (see Cannell, Marquis, & Laurent, 1977, for a good summary, as well as Edwards et al., 1994; Edwards, Winn, & Collins, 1996; Tourangeau, Rips, & Rasinski, 2000).

Respondents answer many questions accurately. For example, more than 90% of overnight hospital stays within 6 months of an interview are reported (Cannell, Marquis, & Laurent, 1977). How well people report, however, depends on both what they are being asked and how it is asked. There are four basic reasons why respondents report events with less than perfect accuracy:

1. They do not understand the question.
2. They do not know the answer.
3. They cannot recall it, although they do know it.
4. They do not want to report the answer in the interview context.

There are several steps that the researcher can take to combat each of these potential problems. These steps are reviewed below.

Understanding the Question

If respondents do not all have the same understanding of what the questions ask for, error is certain to result. As discussed earlier, when researchers are trying to count events that have complex definitions, such as burglaries or physician services, they have two options: (a) Provide definitions to all respondents; or (b) have respondents provide the information needed to classify their experiences into detailed, complex categories, and then have coders categorize answers.

Fowler (1992) has shown that people do answer questions that include ambiguous terms, producing quite distorted data. Researchers cannot assume that respondents will ask for clarification if they are not sure what a question means. To maximize the validity of factual survey data, an essential first step is to write questions that will be consistently understood by all respondents.

Lack of Knowledge

Lack of knowledge as a source of error is of two main types: (a) The chosen respondent does not know the answer to the question, but someone in the selected household does; or (b) no one in the selected household knows the answer. The solution in the first situation lies in choosing the right respondent, not question design. Most often, the problem is that one household respondent is asked to report information about other household members or the household as a whole. Solutions include the following:

- Identify and interview the household member who is best informed.

- Use data collection procedures that permit the respondent to consult with other household members.

- Eliminate proxy respondents; only ask respondents to provide information about themselves.

Sometimes a complex data collection strategy is called for. For example, the National Crime Victimization Survey conducted by the Bureau of the Census obtains reports of household crimes from a single household informant, but in addition asks each household adult directly about personal crimes such as robbery. If the basic interview is to be carried out in person, costs for interviews with other members of the household can be reduced if self-administered forms are left to be filled out by absent household members, or if secondary interviews are done by telephone. A variation is to ask the main respondent to report the desired information as fully as possible for all household members, then mail the respondent a summary for verification, permitting consultation with other family members.

When respondents are asked questions about themselves that they cannot answer, it is a question design problem. In theory, one could differentiate between information the respondent cannot recall and information the respondent never had at all. In either case, the problem for the researcher is to design questions that almost everyone can answer. Among the options available are the following:

* Change the question to ask for information that is less detailed or easier to recall.
* Help the respondent estimate the answer.
* Change or drop the objective.

It is not uncommon for questions to ask for answers in more detail than the research objectives require.

The question asks respondents for the name of all the medications they take (a very hard question) when the objective is to find out who is taking medicine for high blood pressure (a much easier question).

The question asks for income in an open-ended (and implicitly very detailed way) when getting an estimate of income in broad categories would satisfy the research objectives.

Recall follows some obvious principles: Small events that have less impact are more likely to be forgotten than more significant events; recent events are reported better than events that occurred in the more distant past (Cannell, Marquis, & Laurent, 1977). Sometimes it may be worthwhile to change question objectives to improve reporting by asking about events that are easier to recall. For example, although it may be desirable to have respondents report all the crimes that happened in the last year, there will be less reporting error if they are asked to report for only 6 months.

A comparatively new set of question design strategies has resulted from the growing involvement of cognitive psychologists in survey methods (Jabine, Straf, Tanur, & Tourangeau, 1984; Sirken, Herrmann, Schechter, Schwarz, Tanur, & Tourangeau, 1999; Willis, 2005). Various strategies are being tried to help respondents recall events (e.g., by suggesting possible associations) or place events in time (e.g., by having respondents recall something that happened about a year before). Event calendars help respondents place events in time and recall events by putting them in context (Belli, Lee, Stafford, & Chou, 2004).

For many survey tasks, studies have shown that respondents do not actually use recall to answer some questions; they estimate the answers (e.g., Burton & Blair, 1991). For example, if respondents are asked for the number of times they visited a grocery store to buy food in some period, they usually estimate based on their usual patterns rather than try to remember the individual events.

This observation leads researchers to design strategies for helping respondents make better estimates.

Finally, it is important to recognize that there are some things that researchers would like to have people report that they cannot. For example, people do not know the cost of their medical care that is paid by insurance. If one truly wants to obtain medical costs, it is necessary to supplement what respondents may be able to report (for example, their out-of-pocket expenditures) with data collected directly from providers or insurers.

Social Desirability

There are certain facts or events that respondents would rather not report accurately in an interview. Health conditions that have some degree of social undesirability, such as mental illness and venereal disease, are underreported significantly more than other conditions. Hospitalizations associated with conditions that are particularly threatening, either because of the possible stigmas that may be attached to them or because of their life-threatening nature, are reported at a lower rate than average (Cannell, Marquis, & Laurent, 1977). Aggregate estimates of alcohol consumption strongly suggest underreporting, although the reporting problems may be a combination of recall difficulties and respondents' concerns about social norms regarding drinking. Arrest and bankruptcy are other events that have been found to be underreported consistently but seem unlikely to have been forgotten (Locander, Sudman, & Bradburn, 1976).

There are probably limits to what people will report in a standard interview setting. If a researcher realistically expects someone to admit something that is very embarrassing or illegal, extraordinary efforts are needed to convince respondents that the risks are minimal and that the reasons for taking any risk are substantial. The following are some of the steps that a researcher might consider when particularly sensitive questions are being asked (also see Catania, Gibson, Chitwood, & Coates, 1990; Sudman & Bradburn, 1982).

1. *Minimize a sense of judgment; maximize the importance of accuracy.* Careful attention to the introduction and vocabulary that might imply the researcher would value certain answers negatively is important.

Researchers always have to be aware of the fact that respondents are having a conversation with the researcher. The questions and the behavior of the interviewer, if there is one, constitute all the information the respondent has about the kind of interpretation the researcher will give to the answers. Therefore, the researcher needs to be very careful about the cues respondents are receiving about the context in which their answers will be interpreted.

2. *Use self-administered data collection procedures.* Although the data are not conclusive, there is some evidence that telephone interviews are more subject to social desirability bias than personal interviews (Aquilino, 1994; de Leeuw & van der Zouwen, 1988; Fowler et al., 1998; Henson et al., 1977; Mangione et al., 1982). The evidence is much clearer that having respondents answer questions in a self-administered form, on paper or directly into a computer, rather than having an interviewer ask the questions will produce less social desirability bias for some items (e.g., Aquilino, 1994; Aquilino & Losciuto, 1990; Dillman & Tarnai, 1991; Fowler et al., 1998; Hochstim, 1967). For surveys dealing with sensitive topics, a mail survey or group administration should be considered. A personal interview survey also can include some self-administered questions: A respondent simply is given a set of questions to answer in a booklet. If the survey is computer-assisted, the respondents can enter their answers directly into a computer with much the same effect. For example, such an approach has been shown to significantly increase reports of recent illegal drug use (Penne, Lessler, Beiler, & Caspar 1998; Tourangeau & Smith, 1998). Finally, Turner and colleagues (1998) and Villarroel and colleagues (2006) have shown that telephone surveys obtain much higher estimates of socially sensitive activities related to sex and drugs when answers are entered directly into a computer using the touch-tone feature on the telephone than when an interviewer asks the questions.

3. *Assure confidentiality and anonymity.* Almost all surveys promise respondents that answers will be treated confidentially and that no one outside the research staff will ever be able to associate individual respondents with their answers. Respondents usually are assured of such facts by interviewers in their introductions and in advance letters, if there are any; these may be reinforced by signed commitments from the researchers. Self-administered forms that have no identifiers provide a way to ensure that answers are anonymous— not just confidential. Finally, for surveys on particularly sensitive or personal subjects, there are some elaborate survey strategies, such as random response techniques, that respondents cannot be linked to their answers (These are described by Fox & Tracy, 1986, and by Fowler, 1995.)

Again it is important to emphasize that the limit of survey research is what people are willing to tell researchers under the conditions of data collection designed by the researcher. There are some questions that probably cannot be asked of probability samples without extraordinary efforts. Some of the procedures discussed in this section, however, such as trying to create a neutral context for answers and emphasizing the importance of accuracy and the neutrality of the data collection process, are probably worthwhile procedures for the most innocuous of questions. Any question, no matter how innocent it may seem, may have an answer that is embarrassing to somebody in the sample. It is best to design all phases of a survey instrument with a sensitivity to reducing the effects of social desirability and embarrassment for any answers people may give.

INCREASING THE VALIDITY OF ANSWERS
DESCRIBING SUBJECTIVE STATES

As discussed above, the validity of subjective questions has a different meaning from that of objective questions. There is no external criterion; one can estimate the validity of a subjective measure only by the extent to which answers are associated in expected ways with the answers to other questions, or other characteristics of the individual to which it should be related (see Turner & Martin, 1984, for an extensive discussion of issues affecting the validity of subjective measures).

There basically are only three steps to the improvement of validity of subjective measures:

1. Make the questions as reliable as possible. Review the sections on the reliability of questions, dealing with ambiguity of wording, standardized presentation, and vagueness in response form, and do everything possible to get questions that will mean the same thing to all respondents. To the extent that subjective measures are unreliable, their validity will be reduced. A special issue is the reliability of ordinal scales, which are dominant among measures of subjective states. The response alternatives offered must be unidimensional (i.e., deal with only one issue) and monotonic (presented in order, without inversion).

PROBLEMATIC SCALES

6.22   How would you rate your job—very rewarding, rewarding but stressful, not very rewarding but not stressful, or not rewarding at all?

6.23   How would you rate your job—very rewarding, somewhat rewarding, rewarding, or not rewarding at all?

Question 6.22 has two scaled properties, rewardingness and stress, that need not be related. Not all the alternatives are played out. Question 6.22 should be made into two questions if rewardingness and stress of jobs are both to be measured. In 6.23, some would see "rewarding" as more positive than "somewhat rewarding" and be confused about how the categories were ordered. Both of these problems are common and should be avoided.

2. When putting people into ordered classes along a continuum, it probably is better to have more categories than fewer. There is a limit, however, to the precision of discrimination that respondents can exercise in giving ordered ratings. When the number of categories exceeds the respondents' ability to discriminate their feelings, numerous categories simply produce unreliable noise. Also numerous categories may make questions harder to administer, particularly on the telephone. However, to the extent that real variation among respondents is being measured, more categories will increase validity.

3. Ask multiple questions, with different question forms, that measure the same subjective state; combine the answers into a scale. The answers to all questions potentially are influenced both by the subjective state to be measured and by specific features of the respondent or of the questions. Some respondents avoid extreme categories; some tend to agree more than disagree. Multiple questions help even out response idiosyncrasies and improve the validity of the measurement process (Cronbach, 1951; DeVellis, 2003).

The most important point to remember about the meaning of subjective measures is their relativity. Distributions can be compared only when the stimulus situation is the same. Small changes in wording, changing the number of alternatives offered, and even changing the position of a question in a questionnaire can make a major difference in how people answer (see Schuman & Presser, 1981; Sudman & Bradburn, 1982; and Turner & Martin, 1984, for numerous examples of factors that affect response distributions). The distribution of answers to a subjective question cannot be interpreted directly; it only has meaning when differences between samples exposed to the same questions are compared or when patterns of association among answers are studied.

QUESTION DESIGN AND ERROR

A defining property of social surveys is that answers to questions are used as measures. The extent to which those answers are good measures is obviously a critical dimension of the quality of survey estimates. Questions can be poor measures because they are unreliable (producing erratic results) or because they are biased, producing estimates that consistently err in one direction from the true value (as when drunk driving arrests are underreported).

We know quite a bit about how to make questions reliable. The principles outlined in this chapter to increase reliability are probably sound. Although other points might be added to the list, creating unambiguous questions that provide consistent measures across respondents is always a constructive step for good measurement. The validity issue is more complex. In a sense, each variable to be measured requires research to identify the best set of questions to measure it and to produce estimates of how valid the resulting measure is. Many of the suggestions to improve reporting in this chapter emerged from a 20-year program to evaluate and improve the measurement of health-related variables (Cannell, Marquis, & Laurent, 1977; Cannell, Oksenberg, & Converse, 1977). There are many areas in which a great deal more work on validation is needed.

Reducing measurement error through better question design is one of the least costly ways to improve survey estimates. For any survey, it is important to attend to careful question design and pretesting (which are discussed in Chapter 7) and to make use of the existing research literature about how to measure what is to be measured. Also, continuing to build a literature in which the validity of measures has been evaluated and reported is much needed. Robinson, Shaver, and Wrightsman (1997) and McDowell (2003) have compiled data on the validity of many commonly used multi-item measures that document how measures have been validated, as well as how much work remains to be done.

EXERCISES

1. Use the criteria discussed in this chapter to evaluate the following questions as reliable, interpretable, and analytically useful measures; write better questions if you can.

    a. To measure income: How much do you make?

    b. To measure health: How healthy are you?

    c. To measure satisfaction with life: How would you rate your life—very good, better than average, mixed, could be better, or very bad?

    d. To measure opinion about abortion laws: Tell me whether you agree or disagree with the following statement: Abortion is morally very questionable; abortions should be illegal, except in emergencies.

2. Write a series of questions to measure position for or against universal health insurance.

3. Write a series of questions to measure degree of political involvement.

4. Write a hypothesis about a possible relationship between two variables (e.g., good health is associated with receiving good quality health care; or

good quality housing is related to having a high income). Then, under each part of the hypothesis, write the information you would need in order to assign a value to a person for each of the two variables. Then draft a question (or set of questions) for each part, the answers to which would provide the information you need. Indicate whether your questions ask for factual or subjective information and whether the resulting data will have nominal, ordinal, interval, or ratio properties.

Further Readings

Fowler, F. J. (1995). *Improving survey questions.* Thousand Oaks, CA: Sage.

Krosnick, J. A., Judd, C. M., & Wittenbrink, B. (2007). The measurement of attitudes. In D. Albarracin, B. T. Johnson. & M. P. Zanna (Eds.), *The handbook of attitudes* (pp. 21–78). Mahwah, NJ: Lawrence Erlbaum.

Tourangeau, R., Rips, L., & Rasinski, K. (2000). *The psychology of survey response.* Cambridge, UK: Cambridge University Press.

7

Evaluating Survey Questions and Instruments

Designing a good survey instrument involves selecting the questions needed to meet the research objectives, testing them to make sure they can be asked and answered as planned, then putting them into a form to maximize the ease with which respondents and interviewers can do their jobs. This chapter describes steps for designing good survey instruments.

Every survey requires either an interview schedule, which constitutes a script for survey interviewers, or a questionnaire that respondents will read and fill out themselves. These documents, either in paper form or as programs for a computer, will be referred to generically as survey instruments.

Understanding what a good question is and how to use questions as measures, as discussed in Chapter 6, is certainly the foundation of good survey instrument design. There is, however, a series of very practical steps needed to produce a good data collection instrument. This chapter presents a summary of those steps. Converse and Presser (1986), Bradburn and Sudman (1992), Fowler (1995), Groves and colleagues (2004), Presser and colleagues (2004), and Willis (2005) provide longer, more detailed discussions of such steps.

Survey instrument design has two components: deciding what to measure and designing and testing questions that will be good measures. The first step usually is to define the survey objectives, though those objectives may be revised based on subsequent question testing. Then the process of choosing and testing questions takes place. The steps involved in a survey instrument development process may include the following:

- focus group discussions
- drafting a tentative set of questions
- critical review to detect common flaws
- individual cognitive interviews (not replicating proposed data collection procedures)
- putting questions into a survey instrument
- pretesting using an approximation of proposed data collection procedures

DEFINING OBJECTIVES

A prerequisite to designing a good survey instrument is deciding what is to be measured. This may seem simple and self-evident, but it is a step that often is overlooked, to the detriment of the results. One valuable first step is to write a paragraph about what the survey is supposed to accomplish. In designing a survey instrument, researchers often are tempted to add related questions that do not contribute to achieving the project's goals. A check against such temptations is to have a good statement of the purposes, against which the inclusion of a particular area of inquiry can be measured. Second, one should make a list of what should be measured to accomplish the goals of the project. These should not be questions; they should be variables to be measured, listed in categories or areas that make sense.

An analysis plan should be developed to go with the list of variables to be measured. Presumably, a good start already will have been made in connection with the design of the sample. The researcher will have had to think through which subgroups in the population require special estimates. At this point, however, the researcher should refine those ideas, so that there is a clear list of (a) which variables are designed to be dependent variables, for which measures of central tendency (e.g., means or distributions) are to be estimated; (b) which variables are needed as independent variables in order to understand distributions and patterns of association; and (c) which variables may be needed as control or intervening variables to explain patterns observed and to check out competing hypotheses.

These three documents, a statement of purposes, a list of the kinds of variables to be measured, and a draft of an analysis plan, are essential components to developing a survey instrument.

PRELIMINARY QUESTION DESIGN STEPS

Focus Groups

Before writing a draft of a structured set of questions, it almost always is valuable to conduct focused discussions with people who are in the study population about the issues to be studied. The primary purpose of these discussions is to compare the reality about which respondents will be answering questions with the abstract concepts embedded in the study objectives.

Example. The goal is to measure the number of visits to doctors. A group discussion could be focused on what counts as a visit to a doctor. Two key concepts are "visit" and "doctor." Participants could be asked about the various contacts they had related to doctors (e.g., telephone consultations, trips to have X-rays or laboratory tests, inoculations) and whether or not they considered these contacts to be visits. They also could be asked about the various people they contacted related to their health (e.g., psychologists, psychiatrists, physician assistants, ophthalmologists, optometrists, physical therapists) and asked about whether or not they considered these individuals to be doctors.

This discussion alone could provide critical information of at least three types:

1. The kinds of contacts people have that possibly could be considered visits. This information would help the researcher refine the objectives and refine question wording to make it clear what is and is not to be included. For example, do we want to include telephone consultations? If a nurse practitioner is seen in a doctor's office, does that count?

2. What people know. For example, is everyone clear that a psychiatrist is an M.D., but a psychologist is not? What assumptions can be made about people's knowledge and perceptions of the background, training, or credentials of health care providers?

3. Comprehension of some key words or terms. Does the word *doctor* mean an M.D., or is it more generic (like Kleenex), referring to professionals in white coats delivering health-related services? Do alternative terms, such as *health care provider* or *health care professional,* have consistent meaning for respondents?

Focus group discussions are best with six to eight people. The general protocol is to discuss people's perceptions, experiences, and perhaps feelings related to what is to be measured in the survey. The number of groups that are valuable will vary, but virtually every survey instrument will benefit from at least a couple of focus group discussions at an early stage in the survey instrument development process.

Drafting Questions

Armed with a list of what is to be measured, the researcher attempts to find the single question or set of questions needed to create measures of the variables on the list. Many questions, such as those dealing with background or demographic issues, are standard to many surveys. Reviewing the questions in the General Social Survey carried out by the National Opinion Research Center at the University of Chicago may be useful. Many surveys are also available online through the Inter-university Consortium of Political and

Social Research (ICPSR) at the University of Michigan. McDowell (2003) is a valuable resource for those doing health-related surveys. Copies of original survey instruments from any of the major survey organizations also are useful as references. From these, the researcher can glean ideas about how specific questions are phrased, how to generate standardized questions, and how to format survey instruments.

Taking advantage of the work that others have done is very sensible. Of course, it is best to review questions asked by researchers who have done previous work on the study topic. In addition, if questions have been asked of other samples, collecting comparable data may add to the generalizability of the research. The mere fact that someone else has used a question before, however, is no guarantee that it is a very good question or, certainly, that it is an appropriate question for a given survey. Many bad questions are asked over and over again because researchers use them uncritically. All questions should be tested to make sure that they "work" for the populations, context, and goals of a particular study.

PRESURVEY EVALUATION

Critical Systematic Review

Once a set of questions is drafted, a good next step is to subject them to a critical systematic review. Lessler and Forsyth (1996) produced a list of issues to look for in a set of questions. Fowler and Cosenza (2008) also proposed a list of standards for questions that can be applied prior to testing. While neither list is exhaustive, both lists identify a set of question characteristics that are indicative of problem questions. An extension of this has been developed by Graesser and colleagues (Graesser, Cai, Louwerse, & Daniel, 2006), who have a list of 12 question problems that can be identified using an online evaluation tool. Using one of these lists can help to identify questions that need revision; it also can flag issues for attention during the next phases of testing.

Cognitive Laboratory Interviews

Once a set of questions has been drafted, critically reviewed, and revised as warranted, the next step is to find out if they are questions people consistently can understand and can answer. Focus group discussions should provide some insights into comprehension issues, but they do not provide a forum for evaluating specific wording or the difficulty of the response task. At early stages of framing questions, the researcher also can learn a great deal by trying out questions on friends, relatives, and coworkers. Early versions of most survey instruments contain questions that are confusing, that cannot be read as written, and that are virtually unanswerable by anyone.

Once questions are in draft form, but before subjecting them to a formal field pretesting, a more formal kind of testing, commonly called *cognitive testing,* is a valuable next step (DeMaio & Rothgeb, 1996; Forsyth & Lessler, 1992; Fowler, 1995; Lessler & Tourangeau, 1989; Presser et al., 2004; Willis, 2005; Willis, DeMaio, & Harris-Kojetin, 1999). Although cognitive interviews take a variety of forms, there are certain features that they usually share. First, respondents are volunteers who have a willingness to expend more time than the data collection itself actually involves in order to help the researchers understand how the questions work. Often respondents are paid and are brought into a laboratory setting, where the interviews can be observed or videotaped.

These interviews usually are not done by regular interviewers. In some cases, interviewers are cognitive psychologists; in other cases, interviews are done by the investigators themselves or senior interviewer supervisors. In most cases, interviewers are thoroughly knowledgeable about the objectives of each question, so that they can detect issues that arise in the way that respondents understand questions or form answers to questions.

A typical protocol calls for asking respondents a set of proposed questions, then in some way gathering information about how the respondents understood the questions and about the way in which they answered them. Sometimes respondents are asked to "think aloud" while they are preparing their answers. In other cases, respondents are asked a set of follow-up questions about the way they understood each question and about issues related to their answers. Two of the most common tasks are

1. to ask respondents to say in their own words what they think the question is asking

2. to ask respondents to explain how they chose a particular answer over others

The point is to get enough information about the respondents' comprehension and preparation of responses to evaluate whether they performed the task in the way the researcher wanted. There are four specific kinds of questions that most cognitive testing is designed to answer:

1. Are questions consistently understood?

2. Do respondents have the information needed to answer the questions?

3. Do the answers accurately describe what respondents have to say?

4. Do the answers provide valid measures of what the question is designed to measure?

There are limits to what can be learned from laboratory interviews. Usually few such interviews are done (often fewer than 10), because they are labor intensive and, in most organizations, can only be conducted by a small number of people. Second, the interviews are conducted under artificial conditions; tasks that volunteers are able and willing to perform may not be handled by a cross-section sample interviewed in their homes. Nonetheless, such interviews are increasingly seen as an essential step in the design and evaluation of a survey instrument. Questions that are not consistently understood or answered in a laboratory setting certainly will not work any better in an actual survey. Problems of comprehension and difficulties with the response task are not identified as reliably in field pretests as they are in laboratory interviews, where the answering process can be examined.

The cognitive laboratory interview has most often been used to test interview protocols. The same issues of comprehension and difficulty of the response task, however, apply to self-administered forms. Although standard tests of self-administered forms, as described below, often involve debriefing questions similar to those used in cognitive interviews, respondent comprehension is more apparent when the question-and-answer process is carried out orally. Thus, to test questions designed to be self-administered, an oral cognitive interview may be an effective way to identify problems that will not be picked up in the standard pretest.

DESIGN, FORMAT, AND LAYOUT OF SURVEY INSTRUMENTS

Once a set of questions is close to ready for final pretesting, the questions need to be put into a form to facilitate interviewer or self-administration. A first step is simply to order the questions. Many researchers like to start with relatively easy, straightforward questions that help get the respondent into the survey. Questions requiring a good deal of thought, or those believed to be sensitive, often are reserved for the middle or later sections of survey instruments. A good practical step is to number questions in sections: A1, A2, B1, B2, and so forth. In this way, when questions are added or deleted, it is not necessary to renumber every question.

Whether the survey is to be interviewer administered or self-administered, the goal of the layout and format of the questionnaire should be to make the tasks of the interviewer and the respondent as easy as possible. For an interviewer-administered survey instrument, the following are some rules that will help achieve that goal:

1. Adopt a convention that differentiates between the words that interviewers are to read to respondents and words that are instructions. A common

convention is to use uppercase letters for instructions and lowercase for questions to be read aloud.

2. If an interview uses a paper-and-pencil form, and is not computer assisted, establish a clear convention for handling instructions to skip questions that do not apply to a particular respondent. A common convention is to put INSTRUCTIONS IN CAPITAL LETTERS. The instructions should be keyed to a particular response and tell the interviewer where to go to ask the next questions. Of course, computer-assisted instruments will make skips automatically, based on the answers that are entered.

3. Put optional wording in parentheses. Conventions such as (his/her) or (husband/wife) are easy for interviewers to handle smoothly if they are alerted by the parentheses. A similar convention uses all caps (e.g., SPOUSE) when the interviewer must supply a word that is not provided in the question itself. Computer assistance often enables optional wording to be filled in, rather than have the interviewer adapt the wording to the situation.

4. Check to make sure that all the words that an interviewer has to say are, in fact, written. This includes not only the phrasing of the questions but transitions, introductions to questions, needed definitions, and explanations.

For self-administered questionnaires, the same kind of general principles apply; that is, the main goal is to make the questionnaire easy to use. If anything, the formatting of a self-administered questionnaire is more important. In contrast to interviewers, respondents do not receive the benefit of training, they usually are not motivated to do the job well, and they are not selected on the basis of their ability to handle questionnaires. Five guiding principles are as follows:

1. A self-administered questionnaire mainly should be self-explanatory. Reading instructions should not be necessary, because they will not be read consistently.

2. Self-administered questionnaires mainly should be restricted to closed answers. Checking a box, clicking on a response, or circling a number should be the only tasks required. When respondents are asked to answer in their own words, the answers usually are incomplete, vague, and difficult to code, and therefore they are of only limited value as measurements.

3. The question forms in a self-administered questionnaire should be few in number. The more the instrument can be set up so that the respondent has the same kinds of tasks and questions to answer, the less likely it is that respondents will become confused; also, the easier the task will be for the respondents.

4. A questionnaire should be laid out in a way that seems clear and uncluttered. Photo reduction (or other strategies for putting many questions on a

page) actually reduces the response rate compared with when the same number of questions are spaced attractively over more pages.

5. Provide redundant information to respondents by having written and visual cues that convey the same message about how to proceed. If people possibly can be confused about what they are supposed to do, they will be. Work on making everything simple and clear.

Most of the principles outlined above also apply to computer-assisted instruments. In addition, helping respondents and interviewers handle common navigational challenges such as how to correct previous answers or what to do if respondents want to skip a question is an important part of the design work. The key to addressing all these issues is to find the problems through testing. Good descriptions of testing procedure are found in Dillman and Redline (2004), Tarnai and Moore (2004), Hansen and Couper (2004), and Baker, Crawford, and Swinehart (2004).

FIELD PRETESTS

Once a survey instrument has been designed that a researcher thinks is nearly ready to be used, a field pretest of the instrument and procedures should be done. The purpose of such pretests is to find out how the data collection protocols and the survey instruments work under realistic conditions.

Pretesting an Interview Schedule

The traditional pretest done by conscientious survey organizations usually consists of experienced interviewers taking 20 to 50 interviews with respondents drawn from a population the same as, or similar to, the population to be included in the survey. Interviewers are asked to play two roles in such pretests: They are interviewers, carrying out the procedures, and they are observers of the data collection process who are asked to report back to the researchers about any ways in which the procedures and survey instruments could be improved. It probably is most typical for this feedback process to take place in a group debriefing session, though on occasions interviewers report back individually.

Pretests such as those described above are an essential part of the survey design process. A particularly important function is to test the usability of the instrument, both the questions and the layout, from the interviewers' perspective. However, such tests also have several limitations. The standards that interviewers use for what constitutes a problem often are not specified well, and it is almost certain that interviewers are inconsistent in what they consider to be a problem. In addition, a group discussion is an imperfect way to gather systematic information about the pretest experience.

Researchers have added steps designed to make the pretest experience more systematic and more valuable. One simple innovation is to ask interviewers to fill out a brief rating form on each question in addition to reporting back in a group session. One such rating form asks interviewers to evaluate each question with respect to whether or not (a) it is easy to read as worded, (b) respondents understand the question in a consistent way, and (c) respondents can answer the question accurately (Fowler, 1995). Obviously, interviewers have to guess about whether or not respondents are understanding questions and answering accurately; however, they do this in any case. The advantage of a form is that interviewers are asked systematically to attend to these aspects of question design as well as the other, more practical aspects of the survey instrument to which they ordinarily attend. Also, having interviewers do these ratings makes it easier for investigators to summarize interviewer reports and identify question problems in a more consistent way.

A more important, and probably more useful, innovation with respect to the field pretest is the use of audio-recording and behavior coding to evaluate survey questions. With respondent permission, which is almost always granted, it is easy to record pretest interviews done either in person or over the telephone. Trained coders can then listen to those recordings and evaluate problems in the question-and-answer process in a consistent way.

Three behaviors have been shown to be most important in identifying problems with survey questions (Fowler & Cannell, 1996; Oksenberg et al., 1991): (a) whether or not the interviewer reads the question as worded, (b) whether or not the respondent asks for clarification, and (c) whether or not the respondent initially gives an inadequate answer that requires interviewer probing. It has been found that questions consistently produce or do not produce these kinds of behaviors in interviews; that is, there are questions that interviewers consistently misread, that lead respondents to ask for clarification, or that respondents consistently answer in an inadequate way. Such coding does not identify all questions that are not consistently understood by respondents. However, when one of these behaviors occurs in 15% or more of pretest interviews, it has been shown that a question is either highly likely to produce distorted data or distinctively susceptible to interviewer effects (Fowler, 1991; Fowler & Mangione, 1990).

An additional benefit of behavior coding of pretest interviews is that the results are systematic and can be replicated. Thus the question evaluation process is moved beyond the subjective opinions of researchers and interviewers, and concrete, replicable evidence is produced about questions that are inadequate.

Trace files are a third source of information from a pretest of a computer-assisted interview. When an interview is computer-assisted, it is possible to retrieve the actual key strokes interviewers make. Those files can identify places where interviewers have to go back to previous screens and questions. Having to return to previous questions slows down an interviewer and often is a sign that question flow is not well designed. Looking at how "help" functions are used can provide clues to where help is needed and how "useful" various help functions are. Again, a plus of examining trace files is that the results are systematic and quantifiable (Couper, Hansen, & Sadowsky, 1997; Hansen & Couper, 2004).

Pretesting a Self-Administered Questionnaire

If anything, self-administered instruments require more pretesting than interviewer-administered survey instruments, simply because interviewers can solve some problems that the researchers did not solve in the design of the survey instrument. Unfortunately, pretesting a self-administered instrument is also somewhat harder, because problems of comprehension and difficulties with answering questions are less evident. Although people have used observation of how people fill out forms or interact with a computer as a way of trying to identify unclear or confusing questions and instructions, it is not as satisfactory as the audio recording and behavior coding of interviews to identify question problems.

Probably the best way to pretest a self-administered questionnaire is in person, with a group of potential respondents. If it is a computer-based survey, respondents can respond via individual laptops. First, respondents should fill out the questionnaire as they would if they were part of a survey. Then the researcher can lead a discussion about the instrument. One topic obviously is whether the instructions were clear. A second is whether or not the questions were clear. A third is whether there were any problems in understanding what kind of answers were expected or in providing answers to the questions as posed (Dillman & Redline, 2004).

In addition to group tests, the usability of a computer-based instrument often benefits from some one-on-one testing, in which some respondents are observed interacting with the computer and the questions (Tamai & Moore, 2004). Direct observation or videotaping can be use to identify trouble spots. Again, trace files can also be examined to identify navigational problems or places where respondents went back to correct answers.

Debugging a Computer-Assisted Instrument

Having interviewers or respondents test instruments provides information about ease of use, but it does not provide information about whether or not the data collection protocol is correct. The key area for concern is the "skip" instructions.

A great strength of computer assistance is to help respondents and interviews correctly navigate contingencies: when which questions are asked, or how they are worded, is tied to the answers given to preceding questions. Of course, the accuracy of the "skip" instructions requires careful proofreading of the final versions of paper instruments. However, the challenges of checking the accuracy of computer-assisted instruments are much greater than for paper instruments. The problem is that testers cannot see which questions are skipped and, hence, they may miss the fact that a question is skipped that should have been asked. Proofreading a printout of the program and extensive testing are valuable steps. However, if an instrument is long and contains complex contingencies, those steps may be inadequate.

For this reason, once a survey begins, it should be standard practice to tabulate the distributions of answers to the early returns. It is only by checking such output that a researcher can be sure that the contingency instructions are working as intended.

SURVEY INSTRUMENT LENGTH

One outcome of a good pretest is to find out how long it takes to complete a survey instrument. The criteria for interview length should include cost, effect on response rate, and the limits of respondent ability and willingness to answer questions. The extent to which the length of a self-administered questionnaire affects costs and response rates varies with the population being studied and the topic; generalizations are difficult. It also is hard to generalize about how long people can be interviewed.

When researchers find they have more questions to ask than they feel they can ask, there are two choices available. Of course, the researcher simply may cut questions. An alternative approach is to assign subsets of questions to representative subsamples of respondents. Such an approach increases the complexity of the survey and reduces the precision of estimates of those variables, but this may be preferable to leaving out questions altogether. A clear advantage of computer-assisted data collection is the ease with which such designs can be implemented.

CONCLUSION

There was a time when one might have thought that evaluation of questions was largely a subjective process, contingent on the taste and preference of interviewers and researchers. We now know we can move beyond that. Survey questions should mean the same thing to all respondents, answering the questions should be a task that most or almost all respondents can perform, and the words in an interview schedule should be an adequate script that interviewers can follow as worded in order to conduct an interview.

Obviously, no matter how clear the question, some respondents will have difficulty with it, and some interviewers will misread it. There are judgments to be made about how bad a question can be before it must be changed. A critical part of the design and evaluation process of survey instruments, however, is to gather information about comprehension, the task of answering questions, and how interviewers and respondents use the protocols in order that judgments can be made about whether or not the questions and instruments need to be changed. Good question and instrument evaluation prior to actually doing a survey is a critical part of good survey practice. It is one of the least expensive ways to reduce error in survey estimates. Although there is work to be done to define the most efficient and effective ways of evaluating questions, the procedures outlined on the preceding pages constitute a useful array of techniques that, when used, will have a major positive impact on the quality of survey data.

EXERCISES

Take the questions generated in the exercise for Chapter 6 and transform them into a set of questions that an interviewer could administer in a standardized way.

1. Cognitively test the questions and revise as needed.
2. Pretest the resulting questions. Revise as needed.
3. Now put the same questions in a form for self-administration. Pretest that.

Further Readings

Presser, S., et al. (2004). *Methods for testing and evaluating survey questionnaires.* Hoboken, NJ: John Wiley.
Willis, G. (2005). *Cognitive interviewing.* Thousand Oaks, CA: Sage.

8

Survey Interviewing

Interviewers affect survey estimates in three ways: They play a major role in the response rate that is achieved, they are responsible for training and motivating respondents, and they must handle their part of the interview interaction and question-and-answer process in a standardized, nonbiasing way. This chapter discusses the significance of interviewer selection, training, and supervision, plus the procedures interviewers are given, for minimizing interviewer-related error in surveys.

OVERVIEW OF INTERVIEWER JOB

Although many surveys are carried out using self-administered methods, using interviewers to ask questions and record answers is certainly a common part of survey measurement procedures, both face-to-face and over the telephone. Because of the central role they play in data collection, interviewers have a great deal of potential for influencing the quality of the data they collect. The management of interviewers is a difficult task, particularly in personal interviewer studies. The goal of this chapter is to provide an understanding of what an interviewer is supposed to do, appropriate procedures for managing interviewers, and the significance of interviewer management and performance for the quality of survey-based estimates.

Interviewers have three primary roles to play in the collection of survey data:

- to locate and enlist the cooperation of selected respondents
- to train and motivate respondents to do a good job of being a respondent
- to ask questions, record answers, and probe incomplete answers to ensure that answers meet the question objectives

Gaining Cooperation

Interviewers have to get in touch with respondents in order to enlist cooperation. The difficulty of this part of the job differs greatly with the sample.

Interviewers have to be available when respondents want to be interviewed, they have to be available (and persistent) enough to make contact with hard-to-reach respondents, and for in-person interviews in people's homes, they have to be able and willing to go where the respondents are.

Although many sampled individuals agree readily to be interviewed, enlisting the cooperation of uninformed or initially reluctant respondents is undoubtedly one of the hardest and one of the most important tasks interviewers must perform. More interviewers probably fail in this area than any other.

There is no doubt that some interviewers are much better than others at enlisting cooperation. It also is clear that different personal styles will work. Some effective interviewers are very businesslike, whereas others are more casual and personable. Experience suggests that there are two characteristics that interviewers who are good at enlisting cooperation seem to share. First, they have a kind of confident assertiveness. They present the study as if there is no question that the respondent will want to cooperate. The tone and content of their conversation does not hint at doubt that an interview will result. Second, they have a knack of instantly engaging people personally, so that the interaction is focused on and tailored very individually to the respondent. It may be very task oriented, but it is responsive to the individual's needs, concerns, and situation. Reading a predesigned script is not an effective way to enlist cooperation.

Although these interviewer skills are important for all surveys, they are challenged particularly by telephone surveys for which respondents receive no advance notice (as in the case when RDD is used) or when the subject matter does not readily engage respondent interest.

Training and Motivating Respondents

Respondents' performance, such as the accuracy of reporting, has been linked to their orientation to the interview. Interviewers have been shown to play an important role in setting respondent goals (Cannell & Fowler, 1964; Cannell, Oksenberg, & Converse, 1977; Fowler & Mangione, 1990). For example, interviewers who rush through interviews encourage respondents to answer questions quickly. Interviewers who read questions slowly indicate to respondents, in a nonverbal way, their willingness to take the time to obtain thoughtful, accurate answers; consequently, they do obtain more accurate answers. Studies also show that the way interviewers provide encouragement to respondents affects their sense of what they are supposed to do and how well they report (Cannell et al., 1987; Cannell, Oksenberg, & Converse, 1977; Fowler & Mangione, 1990; Marquis, Cannell, & Laurent, 1972).

There is no doubt that most respondents have little idea of what they are expected to do and how they are to perform their roles. Interviewers both explicitly and implicitly teach respondents how to behave; this is an often unappreciated but critical part of the interviewer's job.

Being a Standardized Interviewer

Survey researchers would like to assume that differences in answers can be attributed to differences in what respondents have to say (i.e., their views and their experiences) rather than to differences in the stimulus to which they were exposed (i.e., the question wording, the context in which it was asked, and the way it was asked). The majority of interviewer training is aimed at teaching trainees to be standardized interviewers who do not affect the answers they obtain. There are five aspects of interviewer behavior that researchers attempt to standardize: the way interviewers present the study and the task; the way questions are asked, the way inadequate answers (i.e., answers that do not meet question objectives) are probed, the way answers are recorded, and the way the interpersonal aspects of the interview are handled. Each of these is discussed below in greater detail.

1. *Presenting the study.* Respondents should have a common understanding of the purposes of the study, because this sense of purpose may have a bearing on the way they answer questions. Assumptions about such things as confidentiality, the voluntary nature of a project, and who will use the results also potentially can have some effect on answers. A good interviewing staff will give all respondents a similar orientation to the project so that the context of the interview is as constant as possible.

2. *Asking the questions.* Survey questions are supposed to be asked exactly the way they are written, with no variation or wording changes. Even small changes in the way questions are worded have been shown, in some instances, to have significant effects on the way questions are answered.

3. *Probing.* If a respondent does not answer a question fully, the interviewer must ask some kind of follow-up question to elicit a better answer; this is called *probing*. Interviewers are supposed to probe incomplete answers in nondirective ways—ways that do not increase the likelihood of any one answer over another. For fixed response questions, repeating the question and all the response alternatives is the most commonly needed probe. For open-ended questions, repeating the question, or asking "Anything else?"; "Tell me more?"; or "How do you mean that?" will handle most situations if the survey instrument is designed well.

4. *Recording the answers.* The recording of answers should be standardized so that no interviewer-induced variation occurs at that stage. When an open-ended question is asked, interviewers are expected to record answers verbatim; that is, exactly in the words that the respondent uses, without paraphrasing, summarizing, or leaving anything out. In fixed-response questions, when respondents are given a choice of answers, interviewers are required only to record an answer when the respondent actually chooses one. There is potential for inconsistency if interviewers code respondent words into categories that the respondent did not choose.

5. *Interpersonal relations.* The interpersonal aspects of an interview are to be managed in a standardized way. Inevitably, an interviewer brings some obvious demographic characteristics into an interview, such as gender, age, and education. By emphasizing the professional aspects of the interaction and focusing on the task, however, the personal side of the relationship can be minimized. Interviewers generally are instructed not to tell stories about themselves or to express views or opinions related to the subject matter of the interview. Interviewers are not to communicate any judgments on answers that respondents give. In short, behaviors that communicate the personal, idiosyncratic characteristics of the interviewer are to be avoided because they will vary across interviewers. To behave as a professional, not a friend, helps to standardize the relationship across interviewers and respondents. There is no evidence that having a friendly interpersonal style *per se* improves the accuracy of reporting; it probably tends to have a negative effect on accuracy (Fowler & Mangione, 1990).

A special complexity is introduced when the interviewer and respondent come from different backgrounds in society. In this instance, communication may not be as free and easy as when backgrounds are similar. There is some evidence that interviewers who take steps to ease communication in such situations (e.g., by introducing a bit of humor) may be able to produce a more effective interview (Fowler & Mangione, 1990). Efforts to relax the respondent, however, should not detract from a basically professional interaction, focused on good task performance.

Significance of Interviewer's Job

It should be clear from the above that interviewing is a difficult job. Moreover, failure to perform the job may produce three different kinds of error in survey data:

- Samples lose credibility and are potentially biased if interviewers do not do a good job of enlisting respondent cooperation.

- The precision of survey estimates will be reduced, there will be more error around estimates, to the extent that interviewers are inconsistent in ways that influence the data.

- Answers may be systematically inaccurate or biased to the extent that interviewers fail to train and motivate respondents appropriately or fail to establish an appropriate interpersonal setting for reporting what is required.

Given all this potential to produce error, researchers should be motivated to use good interviewers. There are several avenues for affecting the quality of an interviewer's work: recruitment and selection, training, supervision, designing good questions, and using effective procedures. The next five sections will discuss the potential of each of these to influence interviewer performance.

INTERVIEWER RECRUITMENT AND SELECTION

Some of the characteristics of interviewers are dictated by requirements of the survey interviewer's job that have nothing to do with the quality of data per se:

1. Interviewers must have reasonably good reading and writing skills. Many, if not most, interviewers now work with computers, so that typing skills and general familiarity with computers are usually needed, too. Most survey research organizations require high school graduation, and many require or prefer interviewers to have at least some college experience.

2. Interviewing is primarily part-time work. It is difficult to work 40 hours a week every week on general population surveys; survey organizations almost always have some ebbs and flows of work for interviewers. As a result, potential interviewers usually are people who can tolerate intermittent income or are between more permanent jobs. Interviewer pay is usually not high for a college-educated person. Often, there are no benefits, such as health insurance, to the interviewer job. It is unusual for a survey interviewer to be able to rely on interviewing as a sole source of income and support over a long period of time.

3. Personal household interviewers must have some flexibility of hours; surveys require interviewers to be available when respondents are available. One advantage of telephone interviewing is that individual interviewers can work more predictable shifts, although evening and weekend work is prime time for almost all general-population survey work.

4. Personal household interviewers must be mobile, which often excludes people with some physical disabilities and those without the use of a car. Neither of these restrictions is salient to telephone interviewers.

Beyond these practical job requirements, there is little research basis for preferring one set of interviewer candidates over others. For example, experienced interviewers are likely to be better at enlisting cooperation simply because those for whom it is a problem will not continue to work as interviewers; however, there is no documented positive effect of experience on data quality. There is some evidence that interviewers become careless and collect poorer data over time (Bradburn, Sudman, & Associates, 1979; Cannell, Marquis, & Laurent, 1977; Chromy, Eyerman, Odom, McNeeley, & Hughes, 2005; Fowler & Mangione, 1990; Groves et al., 2004).

Likewise, having interviewers who have specialized knowledge about the subject matter is seldom a plus. In fact, because knowledgeable interviewers may assume they know what the respondent is saying when the respondent has not been clear, they may read more into what the individual is saying than people not trained in the area. Unless interviewer observations or ratings requiring an extensive specialized background are needed, a trained interviewer with no special background usually is the best choice.

Age, education, and gender of interviewer seldom have been associated with data quality, though there is some evidence that females may, on average, be more positively rated by cross-section samples (Fowler & Mangione, 1990; Groves, 1989). In general, a researcher would be best advised to send the best interviewer available to interview a respondent, regardless of demographic characteristics. The exception is if the subject matter of the survey directly bears on race or religion (or any demographic characteristic) and the feelings of the respondents about people in the same or different groups. For example, if people are to be interviewed about their own anti-Semitic feelings, the Jewishness of the interviewer will make a difference in the answers (Robinson & Rhode, 1946). In the same way, blacks and whites express different feelings about race depending on the interviewer's skin color (Schuman & Converse, 1971).

It is important to note, however, that matching on ethnicity does not necessarily improve reporting. Two studies of this issue found that black respondents reported income from welfare (Weiss, 1968) and voting (Anderson, Silver, & Abramson, 1988) more accurately to white interviewers than to black interviewers.

There is no question that a researcher should consider the interaction between the subject matter of a survey and the demographic characteristics of the interviewers and respondents. If ethnicity (or some other characteristic) is extremely salient to the answers to be given, controlling the relationship of interviewer and respondent characteristics should be considered so that the effect of the interviewer on the data can be measured (Groves, 1989). For most surveys, however, the practical difficulties and costs of controlling interviewer assignments and the lack of predictable effects will argue against trying to control the demographic characteristics of respondents and interviewers.

Finally, volunteer interviewing staffs are almost always unsuccessful at carrying out probability sample surveys. There are several reasons for the failure of volunteers. Because it is hard to require attendance at lengthy training sessions, volunteers usually are trained poorly. Because it is hard to terminate poor volunteer interviewers, response rates are usually low. Moreover, volunteer attrition is usually high.

The above discussion offers few guidelines for researchers in the selection of interviewers. In some rather specialized circumstances, the interviewer's ethnic background, age, or gender may affect answers; for example, teenagers may respond differently to older female interviewers (Erlich & Riesman, 1961). For most surveys, however, the particular job requirements largely will dictate the pool of interviewers. There is little basis for ruling out people because of their background or personality characteristics. Rather, the key to building a good interviewing staff is good training and careful supervision. In addition, because of the difficulty of identifying good interviewers in advance, attrition of less able interviewers is probably a critical and necessary part of building a good staff of interviewers.

TRAINING INTERVIEWERS

There is great diversity in the kinds of training experiences to which survey interviewers are exposed. The exact amount of time that will be devoted to training, the kind of training session, and the content of the program obviously will depend on the particular organizational setting and what interviewers are going to be doing. There is some disagreement, in addition, on the extent to which effort should be devoted to an initial training session, prior to the onset of field experience, versus continuous learning and retraining after interviewers have begun. Nonetheless, all professional survey organizations concerned about data quality have at least some kind of (usually face-to-face) training of all new interviewers. The following is a general summary of what reasonable interviewer training might entail.

Content of Training

The content of training includes both general information about interviewing that applies to all surveys and information specific to the particular study on which interviewers are to work. The general topics to be covered will include the following:

- procedures for contacting respondents and introducing the study
- the conventions that are used in the design of the survey instrument with respect to wording and skip instructions, so that interviewers can ask the questions in a consistent and standardized way
- procedures for probing inadequate answers in a nondirective way
- procedures for recording answers to open-ended and closed questions
- rules and guidelines for handling the interpersonal aspects of the interview in a nonbiasing way
- how to use the computer-assisted interviewing programs

In addition, many research organizations feel that it is a good idea to give interviewers a sense of the way that interviewing fits into the total research process. For that reason, they often attempt to give interviewers some familiarity with sampling procedures, coding, and the kinds of analyses and reports that result from surveys. Such information may be helpful to interviewers in answering respondent questions and may play a positive role in motivating the interviewer and helping him or her to understand the job.

With respect to any specific project, interviewers also need to know the following:

- Specific purposes of the project, including the sponsorship, the general research goals, and anticipated uses of the research. This information is basic to providing respondents with appropriate answers to questions and helping to enlist cooperation.

- The specific approach that was used for sampling, again to provide a basis for answering respondent questions. In addition, there may be some training required in how to implement the basic sample design.

- Details regarding the purposes of specific questions—not necessarily their roles in analyses, but at least the kind of information they are designed to elicit.

- The specific steps that will be taken with respect to confidentiality, and the kinds of assurances that are appropriate to give to respondents.

Procedures for Training

There are six basic ways to teach interviewers: written materials, lectures and presentations, computer-based tutorials, planned exercises, practice role-playing, and observation of early interviews. Written materials are usually of two types. First, it is a very good idea to have a general interviewer manual that provides a complete written description of interviewing procedures. In addition, for each particular study, there normally should be some project-specific instructions in writing. It is tempting when interviewers are being trained in person and a project is being done in a local site to skimp on the preparation of written materials. Newly trained interviewers, however, say that there is an overwhelming amount of material and information to absorb during training. Having the procedures in writing enables interviewers to review material at a more leisurely pace; it also increases the odds that messages are stated clearly and accurately.

Lectures and demonstrations obviously have a role to play in any interviewer training, whether only a single interviewer or a large group of interviewers is being trained. In addition to the general presentation of required procedures and skills, most trainers find that demonstrating a standardized interview is a quick and efficient way to give interviewers a sense of how to administer an interview. Videotapes are often used to supplement lectures. Making videotapes of practice interviews or other interviewer activities is a good tool for interviewer training.

The widespread use of computer-assisted interviewing means that interviewer training must include teaching interviewers to use computer-based instruments. The most widely used survey systems have computer-based tutorials that can be integrated into general interviewer training.

Because these are new skills, supervised structured practice is one of the most important parts of interviewer training. Having interviewers take turns playing the respondent and interviewer roles is common practice. Practice should include enlisting cooperation and handling the question-and-answer process. There also is great value in monitoring some practice interviews with respondents who are not role playing and whom interviewers do not know. For personal interviews, supervisors can accompany and observe new interviewers doing practice interviews or review tape-recorded interviews. On the telephone, interviews may be monitored directly or tape-recorded for later review.

Two studies (Billiet & Loosveldt, 1988; Fowler & Mangione, 1990) concluded that interviewer training of less than 1 day produces unsatisfactory interviewers; they are not able to perform their jobs as instructed, and the resulting data are affected adversely. Training programs lasting from 2 to 5 days are the norm in professional survey organizations. The length of training depends on numerous factors, including the number of interviewers to be trained and the complexity of the project for which they are being trained. The critical key to the quality of training, however, is probably the amount of supervised practice interviewing.

SUPERVISION

The keys to good supervision are to have the information needed to evaluate interviewer performance and to invest the time and resources required to evaluate the information and provide timely feedback. There are four main aspects of interviewer performance to supervise: costs, rate of response, quality of completed questionnaires, and quality of interviewing. It is considerably easier to supervise interviewers who are doing telephone interviewing from a centralized facility than those interviewing in households.

Costs

Supervising costs for interviewers requires timely information about time spent, productivity (usually interviews completed), and mileage charges for interviewers using cars. High-cost telephone interviewers are likely to be those who work at less productive times, who have high refusal rates (a refusal takes almost as much time as an interview), or who simply find ways (e.g., editing interviews, sharpening pencils) to make fewer calls per hour. High-cost personal household interviewers are likely to live far from their sample addresses, to make trips that are too short or at the wrong times (evenings and weekends are clearly the most productive), or to have poor response rates.

Response Rates

It is critical to monitor response rates (particularly rates of refusals) by interviewers on a timely basis; however, this is not easy to do. There are three main problems:

1. For personal interviews, but not telephone surveys from a computerized central facility, it can be hard to maintain timely information about interviewer results.

2. Interviewers can understate their refusals by assigning unsuccessful results to other categories.

3. Assignments to in-person interviewers may not be comparable, so that differences in rates of refusals per interviewer may not be consistent indicators of interviewer performance. This issue applies much less to telephone interviewers working in centralized facilities.

Response rates cannot be calculated accurately until a study is over, but special efforts to identify refusals by interviewer during data collection can alert supervisors to problems and are a very important part of interviewer supervision. It is difficult to help an interviewer who has response rate problems. On telephone studies, a supervisor can listen to introductions and provide feedback immediately after the interview (or noninterview) about how the interviewer might be more effective. For household in-person interviewers, the task is more difficult because the supervisor cannot observe the interviewer's approach unless the supervisor accompanies the interviewer on a trip. Thus the supervisor often must be content with listening to the interviewer give a sample introduction.

Supervisors can give helpful hints to interviewers. It is important to make sure interviewers are fully informed about a survey. Having interviewers practice giving concise, clear answers to common questions may be useful. In addition to working on the details of introductions, supervisors may need to address an interviewer's general feeling about approaching people or about the survey project and its value. There are limits, however, to how much retraining will help; there are people who never can attain good response rates. Although it is stressful, one of the most effective ways to keep response rates high is to take ineffective interviewers off a study.

Review of Completed Survey Instruments

When interviewers are using paper-and-pencil instruments, a sample of completed survey instruments should be reviewed to assess the quality of data interviewers are collecting. When reviewing a completed interview, one obviously can look for whether the recording is legible, the skip instructions are followed appropriately, and the answers obtained are complete enough to permit coding. In addition, looking at a completed interview can give a pretty good idea of the extent to which an interviewer is recording respondent answers verbatim, as compared to recording summaries or paraphrases. For computer-assisted interviews, these issues—except for the recording and probing associated with narrative answers—are not relevant.

The Question-and-Answer Process

The quality of interviewing cannot be supervised by reviewing completed survey instruments; they do not tell the supervisor anything at all about the way the interviewer conducted the interview and how those answers were obtained. In order to learn this, a supervisor must directly observe the interviewing process.

A telephone survey from a central facility permits direct supervision of how the interviewer collects the data. A supervisor can and should be available to monitor interviewers at all times. Some centralized systems include the capability of recording all or a sample of interviews. Supervisors should listen systematically to all or parts of a sample of the interviews that each interviewer takes, evaluating (among other things) appropriate introduction of the study, asking questions exactly as written, probing appropriately and nondirectively, and appropriate handling of the interpersonal aspects of the interview. This process works best if a rating form covering these and other aspects of an interviewer's work is completed routinely by a monitor (Cannell & Oksenberg, 1988).

When interviewers are doing studies in respondents' homes or in other distant places, it is more difficult to supervise the question-and-answer process. There are only two ways to do it: A supervisor can accompany an interviewer as an observer, or interviews can be recorded. Without recording or a program of observation, the researcher has no way to evaluate the quality of interviewing. All the most important aspects of the measurement process are unmonitored. Poor interviewers cannot be identified for retraining, and the researcher cannot report the quality of interviewing beyond saying that the interviewers were told what to do. Indeed, from the interviewer's point of view, it must be difficult to believe that standardized interviewing is important when it is the focus of training but is not attended to further.

Fowler and Mangione (1990) present evidence that personal interviewers are less likely to interview the way they are trained if their work is not monitored directly by tape recording. Both Fowler and Mangione and Billiet and Loosveldt (1988) found that data quality was improved when interviewers were monitored directly in this manner. It is now clear that direct supervision of the interview process should be a part of a well-managed survey. The fact that laptop computers can be set up to audio-record interviews makes it quite feasible to review interviewer behavior.

SURVEY QUESTIONS

Although training and supervision are important to producing good interviewing, perhaps the most important step a researcher can take to produce good interviewing is to design a good survey instrument. Research has shown that certain questions are misread consistently, whereas others consistently are answered inadequately, requiring interviewers to probe to obtain adequate answers (Fowler, 1991; Fowler & Cannell, 1996; Fowler & Mangione, 1990; Oksenberg et al., 1991). These questions can be identified with the kind of pretesting described in Chapter 7.

The more interviewers have to probe, explain, or clarify, the more likely they are to influence answers. The better the survey instrument, the more likely it is that the interviewer will conduct a good, standardized interview. The role of good question design in producing good interviewing is discussed in detail in Fowler and Mangione (1990) and Fowler (1991).

INTERVIEWING PROCEDURES

Training and Motivating Respondents

Studies have demonstrated the value of going beyond good question design to help standardize the interview (Cannell et al., 1987; Cannell, Oksenberg, & Converse, 1977; Miller & Cannell, 1977). For example, the researcher can help the interviewer train the respondent in a consistent way. Before the interview begins, the interviewer might read something like the following:

> Before we start, let me tell you a little bit about the interview process, since most people have not been in a survey like this before. You will be asked two kinds of questions in this survey. In some cases, I will be asking you to answer questions in your own words. In those cases, I will have to write down every word you say, not summarizing anything. For other questions, you will be given a set of answers, and you will be asked to choose the one that is closest to your own view. Even though none of the answers may fit your ideas exactly, choosing the response closest to your views will enable us to compare your answers more easily with those of other people.

Interestingly, interviewers like this instruction a great deal. It explains the respondents' task to them, and it makes the question-and-answer process go more smoothly. In fact, good interviewers give instructions such as these on their own. The value of providing explicit instructions is that it reduces differences among interviewers by having them all do the same thing. In addition, such instructions have a salutary effect on the interviewer's performance. Once the interviewer has read an instruction explaining the job expectations, it is easier to do the job the way it should be done, and it is a little harder to do it wrong, because the respondent now also knows what the interviewer is supposed to do (Fowler & Mangione, 1990).

Standardized instructions to respondents also can be used to set goals and standards for performance:

> It is very important that you answer as accurately as you can. Take your time. Consult records if you want. Ask me to clarify if you have any question about what is wanted.

Such statements ensure that respondents have a common understanding of their priorities. Some interviewers unintentionally promise respondents they will make it easy on respondents if the latter will just give the interview; interviewers who hurry communicate that speed is more important than accuracy. When an instruction such as the above is read, it forces accuracy and data quality to be a central part of the role expectations for both respondent and interviewer. One more source of between-interviewer variability is reduced, and the odds of good performance by both are increased.

In conclusion, there are critical parts of the interviewer's job besides the direct question-and-answer process. In particular, the interviewer is responsible for communicating to the respondent how the interview is to proceed: what the respondent is supposed to do, what the interviewer is going to do, and what their joint goals are. This aspect of the interviewer's job mainly has been left up to the interviewer, and not surprisingly, interviewers differ in how they do it in ways that affect data. By developing standardized instruction programs for respondents, researchers can make the job of the interviewer easier, reduce an important source of between-interviewer variance, and improve the extent to which interviewers and respondents behave in ways that will make the measurement process go better.

Standardized Wording

It was stated previously that asking questions exactly as worded is a foundation of standardized measurement, but not everyone agrees (Tanur, 1991). Critics of standardized interviewing have observed that some questions are not consistently understood by all respondents. When that is the case, they argue that it would produce better data if interviewers were free to clarify or explain the meaning of the question (e.g., Conrad & Schober, 2000; Schober & Conrad, 1997). In a similar vein, critics note that some data collection tasks—for example, when the same information is being gathered about several different people or events—produce very stilted or awkward interactions when interviewers try to use only scripted wording. In these instances, it is argued that giving interviewers more flexibility with wording would result in a more comfortable interviewer–respondent interaction (Schaeffer, 1992).

Some of the criticism of standardized interviewing is primarily the result of poorly designed questions (see Houtkoop-Steenstra, 2000; Suchman & Jordan, 1990). When questions are unclear or provide awkward scripts for interviewers, the solution often is to write better questions, not to have interviewers redesign the questions (Beatty, 1995). There is real basis for concern that when interviewers are given flexibility to reword or explain the questions, they will do it in a way that changes the meaning of questions and makes the resulting

data worse, not better (Fowler & Mangione, 1990). However, there are certain
questions—such as repetitive series or when a few respondents need detailed
definitions that would be cumbersome to provide to all respondents—that
might be better handled by giving interviewers more flexibility. Moreover,
when interviewers make changes in question wording it has not consistently
been shown to increase interviewer-related error or response error (Dykema,
Lepkowski, & Blixt, 1997; Fowler & Mangione, 1990).

There have been some experiments giving interviewers more discretion
about how to ask and probe questions (Conrad & Schober, 2000; Schober &
Conrad, 1997). To date the results have been mixed: the accuracy of some
reports may be improved, but considerably increased interviewer training and
sometimes longer interviews are involved. When and how to give interviewers
more flexibility is a topic that warrants further experimentation. Meanwhile, for
most surveys, designing questions that interviewers can and will ask exactly as
worded remains the primary way to conduct a good survey.

VALIDATION OF INTERVIEWS

The possibility that an interviewer will make up an interview is a potential
concern. The likelihood of this happening varies with the sample, the interviewing staff, and the field procedures. For the most part, concern about validation is restricted to surveys in which interviewers are conducting interviews
in respondents' homes or are doing telephone interviews from their own
homes. In such cases, the actual collection of data is not observable by supervisors. The number of hours to be devoted to carrying out an interview is often
sufficient to motivate an interviewer to make up an interview rather than take
the time and effort to carry it out.

In the long run, probably the best protection against faked interviews is to
have a set of interviewers that have some commitment to the quality of the
research and the organization. Such problems seem to occur most often with
newly hired interviewers. Even organizations with an experienced, professional staff, however, routinely check a sample of interviews to make sure they
actually were taken.

There are two approaches to this type of validation. One approach is to mail
all respondents a brief, follow-up questionnaire asking about reactions to the
interview. Probably a more common procedure is to have interviewers obtain
a telephone number from every respondent; a sample is called by a supervisor.
Simply knowing in advance that a validation by mail or telephone will be done
is likely to be a deterrent to interviewer cheating. In addition, to be able to say
that such a check was done may be reassuring to users of the data.

THE ROLE OF INTERVIEWING IN SURVEY ERROR

As noted at the onset of this chapter, interviewers affect response rates, the accuracy of reporting, and the consistency or precision of measurement. Each of these has a central role in the quality of a survey estimate. One of the most observable effects of good survey management is the response rate. Although this issue is discussed more thoroughly in Chapter 4, it is worth repeating that the quality of an interviewing staff is critical to the rate of response that will be obtained in any particular survey.

It is more difficult to measure the error introduced by interviewers in the question-and-answer process. Often survey error is undetectable. When asking questions about subjective states, objective checks for bias or inaccuracy are generally not meaningful, as was discussed in Chapter 6. There have been studies, however, in which researchers had objective measures of facts respondents were asked to report, permitting evaluation of the accuracy of reporting. In one such study (Cannell, Marquis, & Laurent, 1977), samples of households in which someone had been hospitalized in the year preceding were interviewed. The accuracy of reporting could be evaluated by comparing the health interview reports of hospital stays with hospital records. One measure of reporting accuracy was simply the percentage of known hospitalizations that was reported.

In this study, it was found that the number of interviews assigned to an interviewer correlated very highly ($r = .72$) with the percentage of hospitalizations that were unreported in the interview. Interviewers who had large assignments, with whatever pressures that brought to bear on them, collected much less accurate data than those with small assignments.

A different study using the same criterion (the percentage of hospitalizations reported; Cannell & Fowler, 1964) reached a similar conclusion. In this case, half of an interviewer's respondents reported hospitalizations in an interview, whereas the other half completed a self-administered form regarding hospitalizations after the interviewer had completed the rest of the health interview. It was found that interviewers whose respondents reported with great accuracy when asked to report hospitalizations in the interview also had respondents who reported very well in the self-administered form after the interviewer had left ($r = .65$). This study suggested not only that interviewers had a critical role to play in affecting the error of their respondents reporting, but also that one way in which interviewers affected respondent performance was the degree to which they motivated respondents to perform well. In both cases, the effect of the interviewer on reporting accuracy was clear.

In the absence of validating data, one cannot assess accuracy. However, it is possible to assess the extent to which interviewers influence the answers of their respondents. If an interviewing staff operated in a perfectly standardized way, one would be unable to explain any variation in answers by knowing who the interviewer was. To the extent that answers are predictable in part from knowing who did the interview, it can be concluded that the interviewer is inappropriately influencing answers. Groves (1989) thoroughly discusses the techniques for calculating the extent to which interviewers were affecting the answers to questions and summarizes the results of numerous studies in which interviewer effects were calculated. It turns out that for many questions that interviewers ask, one cannot see any effect of the interviewer on the answers. For between one third and one half of the questions in most surveys, however, interviewers significantly affect the answers.

The result of these interviewer effects is to increase the standard errors around survey estimates. The size of the multiplier depends on the size of the intraclass correlation (rho) and on the average size of interviewers' assignments (see Groves, 1989; Kish, 1962). If the intraclass correlation is .01 (which Groves found to be about the average), and the average number of interviews per interviewer is about 31, the standard errors of means will be increased by 14% over those estimated from the sample design alone. When interviewer assignments average closer to 50, for items with an intraclass correlation of .02, the estimates of standard errors will be increased by 41%.

Out of this discussion there are several points to be made about the role of the interviewer in the total error structure of survey data:

1. In addition to their role in response rates, interviewers can be associated with the extent to which respondents give inaccurate answers in surveys and with measurement inconsistency. Existing evidence clearly indicates that interviewers are a significant source of error for many kinds of measures.

2. The training and supervision that interviewers receive can significantly increase the consistency of interviewers, thereby improving the reliability of estimates, and reduce bias. In particular, interviewers who receive minimal training (e.g., less than 1 day) and interviewers who receive minimal or no feedback about the quality of their interviewing are poorer interviewers.

3. Procedures that structure the training and instruction of respondents, minimize inappropriate interviewer feedback, and in general, control more of the interviewer's behavior can reduce interviewer effects on data and increase overall accuracy.

4. Better question design is a key to better interviewing.

5. One design option that has been underappreciated is the size of the average interviewer assignment. Although training and management costs may be

lower if fewer interviewers are used, researchers may pay a price in data reliability for allowing individual interviewers to take large numbers of interviews. Reducing average interviewer assignments often is a cost-effective way to increase the precision of survey estimates.

6. Virtually all reports of the reliability of survey estimates ignore the effects of interviewers on data. In part, this is because researchers cannot sort out interviewer effects from sampling effects when interviewers are assigned samples on a nonrandom basis, such as convenience or geographic proximity. Interviewer effects are a significant source of error, however, for many items in most surveys. Any report of the precision of a survey estimate that ignores interviewer effects is likely to be an underestimate of survey error.

In conclusion, the role of the interviewer in contributing to error in survey data has not been appreciated generally. Although most survey researchers know that some training is necessary for interviewers, procedures for training and supervising interviewers vary widely and often are not adequate. It is unusual for researchers to make any efforts beyond training and supervision to minimize interviewer effects. Yet, these aspects of survey design constitute some of the most cost-effective ways to improve the quality of survey data. The impact of the interviewer on survey estimates deserves a central place in the design and reporting of survey studies that it has not yet achieved.

EXERCISES

1. Tape-record some role-played interviews in which you and/or others use a standardized interview schedule (the questions developed in Chapter 6, or a schedule from another source). Then listen to the tapes and systematically evaluate interviewer performance by noting for each question at least the following errors: did not read question exactly as worded; probed an inadequate answer in a biasing (directive) way; failed to probe an unclear answer; or any other possibly biasing or unstandardized interpersonal behavior. The evaluations are particularly instructive if done by a group, so that interviewer errors can be discussed.

2. Perform a similar exercise role playing an interviewer trying to enlist the cooperation of a potential respondent for an interview.

Further Readings

Fowler, F. J., & Mangione, T. W. (1990). *Standardized survey interviewing: Minimizing interviewer-related error.* Newbury Park, CA: Sage.

9

Preparing Survey Data for Analysis

Survey answers usually are transformed into data files for computer analysis. This chapter describes options and good practice for data formats, code development, coding procedures and management, data entry, and data checking procedures.

Once data have been collected by a survey, no matter what the methods, they almost invariably must be translated into a form appropriate for analysis by computer. This chapter is about the process of taking completed questionnaires and survey interviews and putting them into a form that can be read and processed by a computer. The process of coding or data reduction involves five separate phases:

- deciding on a format (the way the data will be organized in a file)
- designing the code (the rules by which a respondent's answers will be assigned values that can be processed by machine)
- coding (the process of turning responses into standard categories)
- data entry (putting the data into computer readable form)
- data cleaning (doing a final check on the data file for accuracy, completeness, and consistency prior to the onset of analysis)

There are two kinds of errors that can occur in going from an answer to an entry in a data file. First, there can be transcription or entry errors any time someone records an answer or number. Second, there can be coding decision errors, misapplications of the rules for equating answers and code values. The options for quality control are tied to the particular data collection, data entry, and coding procedures chosen. Those options and various alternative procedures are discussed below.

FORMATTING A DATA FILE

The term *record* as used here refers to all the data that pertain to a single individual case or interview. A record can consist of one or more lines of data.

Although conventions and rules vary with facilities and the programs to be used, the following are some common issues:

1. A serial identifier for each respondent usually goes in the same location on each line of data for a particular questionnaire or interview, usually at the beginning of a record. It also helps in checking for the completeness of data files to have a line number in the same location of each line of data if there are multiple lines. These markers preserve the order of the data if they are sorted and are critical for checking files for completeness.

2. It eases coding, data entry, and programming tasks if the data are coded in the order that they appear in the survey instrument. This will reduce errors at these stages and represents a relatively cost-free means of quality control.

3. Multiple codes in a single field or column are acceptable to some computer programs, but not to others. It probably is best to put a single positive entry in each field that contains data. Similarly, some computer programs interpret blanks as zeros, whereas others do not. If zero is meant, it is best actually to code a zero rather than leave a blank field; if the intention is to have a code for item nonresponse, when no codable answer was given, some specific value should be used.

CONSTRUCTING A CODE

A code is a set of rules that translate answers into numbers and vice versa (some systems accept alphabetic values, but the vast majority of codes in surveys use numeric codes only). Which numbers go with which answers is irrelevant to the computer. It is critical to reliable coding and appropriate interpretation of data, however, that the code be unambiguous. There should be a clear rule for what number to assign to each and every answer (or other result). In addition, codes can be designed to minimize errors during coding and analysis. The following are some common principles:

1. Be sure to have missing data codes for questions that are not answered. Codes should differentiate among the following:

   a. *Not ascertained* information, where codable information was not obtained as a result of imperfect interviewer or respondent performance.

   b. *Inapplicable* information, where the information does not apply to a particular respondent because of previous answers (e.g., the data field for length of hospitalization would be coded as "not applying" for those not hospitalized).

   c. *"Don't know"* answers, which may be treated as not ascertained or as a distinct category of missing data.

   d. *Refused to answer,* which may get its own code, as some researchers like a
separate code to differentiate respondent refusals to answer a question from
questions unanswered for other reasons. Others simply treat a refusal to
answer as a "not ascertained" result.

   2. Be consistent in assigning numbers; always use the same code for "not
ascertained," "inapplicable," "don't know," and "other" responses. The more
consistent the code, the fewer the errors coders and programmers will make.

   3. Make codes fit numbers in the real world when possible. Code numbers
exactly (e.g., code a 45-year-old as 45). Also, number a list of responses in
the order they appear in the instrument if there is no compelling reason to do
otherwise.

   When response alternatives are provided to respondents or the response form
is highly structured, the code constructor's job is simply to assign numbers to
the given set of answers and account for missing data. Often response alternatives are prenumbered in the survey instrument. When respondents are asked
to answer questions in their own words, however, the range of answers will not
be fully predictable ahead of time. For such open-response questions, code
development is an interactive process whereby the researcher identifies categories that emerge from the answers, as well as imposing order on the answers
that are obtained.

   The idea is to create categories that group answers that are analytically similar and to differentiate between answers that are different. If the categorization is too fine, the result will be many categories with only a few entries,
which are hard to analyze and waste coder effort. On the other hand, large,
gross categories may mask important differences.

   One critical criterion for a good code is that it must unambiguously assign
each answer to one and only one code number. The other criterion is that it
puts answers in analytically meaningful categories. How well the latter standard is met can be assessed only in the context of a plan for analysis.

   In order to construct such a code:

• Have a clear idea about what characteristics of answers are of analytic significance. A good first step is to jot down the kinds of differences among
answers to each question that are important from the researcher's point of view.

• Actually tabulate some of the answers from early responses. Then construct a draft code for classifying those answers.

• Try the classification scheme on another 10 or 20 returns; revise as
needed.

- Have a separate code for "other" responses that do not fit the categories clearly, and have coders make notes when recording these answers. The notes can be used to expand and clarify the code or add needed categories, as well as providing a record of answers included in the "other" category.

- The same kind of note should be used to allow coders to communicate problems or ambiguities in the coding rules to the researcher, who in turn should refine the definitions and policies.

These steps, together with an effective check-coding operation (discussed below), should produce an exhaustive and nonoverlapping categorization system that unambiguously puts each answer into one and only one place and that can be shared by coders, coding supervisors, and researchers who will analyze the data.

APPROACHES TO CODING AND DATA ENTRY

Some surveys are done using paper-and-pencil instruments. Respondents answer questions by checking boxes or writing in narrative answers; interviewers record the answers that respondents provide in a parallel way. Coding and data entry are the steps by which these answers are turned into numeric electronic data files.

Interviewer recording. There is no practical way to check whether or not interviewers record each and every answer accurately (e.g., check the right box or click the right answer). It is good practice, though, to minimize the extent to which interviewers have to make coding decisions. If response alternatives are not provided, open-response answers are best recorded verbatim to be coded by trained, supervised coders, rather than having interviewers classify narrative answers into categories during an interview (see Houtkoop-Steenstra, 2000).

Coding. Quality control of coding includes the following:

- Train coders, including having all coders code several of the same survey returns and then comparing results to make sure they are all coding the same way.
- Have another coder independently check code a sample of each coder's work. This serves two purposes: it identifies coders who are making coding decision errors, and it identifies coding rules that are ambiguous and require clarification.

- A procedure should be established for coders to write notes about answers they are not certain they know how to code. These notes should be routinely reviewed by a supervisor. Such notes are an extension of the check coding system, helping supervisors identify coders or codes in need of attention and coding rules that require clarification.

Data Entry. Answers collected in paper-and-pencil form are best entered into a data file using one of a number of available data entry programs. In addition to collecting the entries in an organized way so the data can be analyzed, these programs can provide quality control such as:

- permitting the entry of only legal codes in any particular field
- checking entries to make sure they are consistent with other previously entered data
- automatically ensuring that contingency questions are handled appropriately (i.e., when a series of questions is asked only of a subset of respondents, contingency instructions can be programmed so that fields for questions to be skipped will be filled automatically with the proper codes)

Although these checks do not identify data entry errors that do not violate the programmed rules, many data entry errors will be caught at a time when they can be corrected readily. In addition, to the extent that checks for illegal entries, inconsistent data, and conformance with contingency rules are done at the time of data entry, it reduces the need for a very time-consuming and error-prone data cleaning process after the data entry is complete.

Many survey organizations routinely have all data entry independently verified; that is, another staff person, blind to the initial data entry, enters the same data, and any discrepancies can be flagged and errors corrected. This step can make the data entry process virtually error free. If coding and data entry are done as one step, verification becomes a quality control step for both.

The majority of survey data are collected and entered in a one-step process, known as computer-assisted telephone interviewing (CATI), computer-assisted personal interviewing (CAPI), or computer-assisted self-interview (CASI), whereby interviewers or respondents enter answers directly into the computer in a precoded form. Paper and pencil are not used. Collecting data at an Internet site is essentially the same from a data entry perspective as CASI.

For telephone interviews, each interviewer has a terminal at the telephone station. The question appears on the screen, the interviewer reads it, the respondent answers, and the interviewer enters the numerical value that corresponds with the answer into the terminal. That entry triggers a new question on the computer screen. Laptops or other portable personal computers offer the same options for household interviewers. For CASI or when surveys are done via the Internet, the experience is exactly the same except the respondents enter their own answers rather than having an interviewer as an intermediary. In all of these applications, the computer can be programmed to accept only legal entries and to check the consistency of any entry with previously entered data, so that apparent inconsistencies in answers can be dealt with at the time of data collection.

Another technology worth noting is that telephone respondents can enter their answers directly into a data file by using the touchtone feature of their telephones. (For example, "Please press 1 if your answer is yes and 2 if your answer is no.") This is called telephone-audio computer-assisted self-interviewing (T-A CASI). Questions can be asked by a prerecorded computer voice, so no interviewer needs to be involved. Voice recognition systems can be used instead of touchtone data entry. Obviously these approaches are best suited to questions with fixed responses.

A final approach to entering survey data that uses neither interviewers nor data entry staff is optical scanning. There are two ways that scanning is used to enter data.

Response alternatives can be bar coded, so that a person can enter numbers by passing a scanner over a bar next to the chosen response. The advantage of that approach is that a person without data entry skills can enter data, but it still requires a person to manage the data entry.

Optical scanning of special sheets or forms, such as those used for standardized tests, have been available for years and does not require data entry staff. As a result, the data entry costs are very low. The costs mainly are in acquiring the equipment and, if special purpose forms are needed, in setting up and printing the forms.

Historically, there have been downsides to optical scanning for use in surveys:

The forms were not user friendly, and survey researchers want questionnaires to be as easy to use as possible.

Creating special-purpose forms for relatively small surveys is fairly costly.

Significant missing data can result, particularly when unmotivated or unskilled respondents carelessly mark their answers.

The last problem can be handled by having sight checks of missing items to identify marks that the machines could not read. However, the promise for wider use of optical scanners in surveys probably lies in improved technology. Modern scanners are much more tolerant of imperfect marks than those in the past. They also can be used with a variety of formats, making them more adaptable to user-friendly survey instruments.

Scanning only works well with fixed-choice, precoded data, though progress is being made so written answers can be scanned for later coding by a coder. While the best equipment is still comparatively expensive, scanners are likely to play an increasing role in data entry in the future. Dillman and Miller (1998), Dillman (2007), and Blom and Lyberg (1998) provide good summaries of current scanning options and limitations.

To summarize, there are several attractions to all computer-based data collection systems:

1. The computer can follow complex question patterns that are difficult for interviewers or respondents in a paper-and-pencil version of a survey.
2. Information from previous questions or even previous interviews can be taken into account in question wording or the sequence of questions asked.
3. If inconsistent data are given, they are flagged and can be corrected immediately.
4. Data can be added to a data file ready for immediate analysis.

The biggest downside of such systems, compared to paper forms, may be the lead time needed to program a computer-assisted protocol. The program must be error free if it is to be useful. Interviewers cannot deal with programming errors during an interview, as they can with typographical errors in a written schedule, and, of course, errors are even more problematic when respondents are entering their answers directly. Hence considerable time for testing and debugging must be allowed before starting to collect data, though simple instruments with few skips will pose fewer problems for detecting program errors.

In addition, there is no quality control over data entry. There can be no checks on any data entry or on any coding decisions that interviewers make with a computer-assisted system, except to make sure that entries are legal codes and are internally consistent. Although keying error rates are relatively low, the greater concern is the quality of coding decisions (Dielman & Couper, 1995). Because of concerns about the lack of control over coding decisions, when open-response questions are asked, CATI and CAPI interviewers often record the answers verbatim into the computer for later coding. Nichols, Baker, and Martin (1997) and particularly the volume edited by Couper, et al. (1998) provide good summaries of the characteristics, uses, and experience with computer-assisted systems.

DATA CLEANING

Once interviews have been coded and the data entered onto a tape or disk file, the data need to be checked. The most important check is to make sure the data file is complete and in order. In addition, every field should be checked to make sure that only legal codes occur. Even if there were checks built in at the time of data entry, it is good practice to make sure everything worked as planned by running a set of overall distributions. Of course, if checks were not done at the time of data entry, checks for internal consistency should be done as well. When errors are found, the original source must be consulted and corrections made. (Note that this usually is not possible with a CATI, CAPI, or CASI system, because no hard copy is retained of the responses.) Because errors will be made during the correction process, checks should be run again. With large files, this kind of cleaning process is time consuming and error prone. To the extent that errors can be caught at data entry, the reliance on postentry cleaning is reduced, which is highly desirable.

CODING AND DATA REDUCTION AS SOURCES OF ERROR

Because coding and data reduction can take place in a highly supervised setting and can be checked thoroughly, there is the potential to have it be an almost error-free part of the survey process. Moreover, the costs of coding and data reduction usually should be a small fraction of the total survey cost.

When dealing with closed answers, the rate of error from data entry should be much less than 1%. The level of error in the final data will be lower, of course, when those numbers are entered directly and 100% verified, so the transcription process itself is checked.

The reliability of coding open-ended opinion responses will vary with the quality of the question, the quality of the code, and the training and supervision of coders. If a researcher has a reasonably focused question, and if code categories are conceptually clear, one should expect coding to exceed 90% in reliability; that is, the coder and check-coder will disagree in the classification of fewer than 1 out of 10 answers. Coders who are not trained and check-coded appropriately create errors at considerably higher rates. Codes that depend on knowing complete definitions, such as occupational categories, health conditions, or specific legal definitions of crimes, may warrant special attention to coder training and check-coding.

The process of data entry can be nearly error free if it is verified. Although some individual operators are able to enter data at a remarkable level of accuracy, with error rates below 1 in 1,000 entries, one cannot routinely assume that data entry will occur at that level of accuracy.

The choice of the coding and data entry process will often be made for reasons other than the minimization of coding and data entry errors. The speed of file construction and the opportunity to catch errors during the interview are among the appeals of the CATI and CAPI systems, as are some of the strengths of involving a computer in specifying the wording and order of questions. Purely from the perspective of error reduction, however, the two-step process, whereby coders directly enter data and their work (coding and data entry) is 100% verified, may be optimal when a survey involves a significant number of coding decisions. No other system provides a true independent check on all coding decisions, as well as all data entry.

10

Analyzing Survey Data

Once data have been collected and a data file created, the next step is to analyze the data to make statistical estimates and reach conclusions. This chapter is designed to familiarize readers with four analytic issues that most users of survey data have to address in order to analyze their data: adjusting for nonresponse to the survey, adjusting for items that were not answered, weighting to adjust for different probabilities of selection, and calculating the effects of the sample design on the statistical calculations.

ADJUSTING FOR SAMPLE NONRESPONSE AND SAMPLE FRAME DEFICIENCIES

Virtually every survey fails to collect data from or about all the sampled individuals. Also, it is not uncommon for the sample frame used to imperfectly include the entire population the researchers want to describe. Of concern, of course, is the extent to which those not responding or who never had a chance to be selected are different from those who do respond with respect to variables the survey attempts to estimate.

If there is information available about nonrespondents' values, then corrections in the survey estimates can be made directly. However, that is seldom the case, as there would be little need for conducting a special-purpose survey if the information was already available from other sources.

A more common situation is that some information is available about non-respondents, but not about the key variables being estimated. When a sample is drawn from a list, sometimes information is available about every individual selected prior to the survey—most often demographic characteristics such as age, gender, and perhaps race. For samples drawn from general populations, there may be aggregate information available about the whole population. From such data, one can determine whether certain groups are over- or under-represented in the sample of people from whom data were collected.

If one concluded that certain population subgroups were not properly represented in a data set, an obvious question is whether or not estimates could be improved by adjusting the sample data to look more like the population as a whole.

Example: Suppose a population is known to include approximately equal numbers of males and females, but the sample of those responding included 60% females. Females responded to the survey at a higher rate than males, and, hence, men are underrepresented in those responding. One could multiply all the responses of males by 1.5, resulting in responses from males and females getting equal weight, as they would if they had responded at the same rate and the sample perfectly reflected the population.

Consider a survey that yielded 400 respondents, 240 females and 160 males. Suppose each response from a male was weighted 1.5, while responses of females were given a weight of 1.0. This approach would give the 160 males (1.5 × 160 = 240) the same weight as the 240 females. Hence, in the analysis, the representation of the responses of males and females in the data would be the same.

Why would one want to do that? Let's further suppose that one purpose of the survey was to estimate how many drinks respondents usually had on days when they drank alcoholic beverages. Suppose that female respondents reported that they had an average of 2 drinks on days when they drank alcohol, whereas the men reported an average of 4 drinks.

If the data are not weighted, the estimate of the average number of drinks overall is calculated as follows:

240 × 2 = 480, the total number of drinks reported by the females

160 × 4 = 640, the total number of drinks reported by the males

480 + 640 = 1,120, the total number of drinks reported by all

1,120 drinks divided by 400, the number of respondents = 2.8, the average number of drinks reported by those in the sample.

HOWEVER

If we weighted the males' answers so that they are represented in the sample data in the same way they are in the population, we would get

1.5 × 160 × 4 = 960, the number of drinks reported by males (who are now being counted as 240 respondents to adjust for the 80 males who did not respond but would have if they had had the same response rates as the females)

480 + 960 drinks = 1,440, the number of drinks reported by the males and females (with male responses weighted by 1.5)

1,440 drinks divided by 480 responses (the females plus 1.5 of the males) = 3.0, the estimated average number of drinks for the whole population

By weighting the analysis to adjust for the fact that females responded to the survey at a higher rate than males, we changed the estimate from 2.8 to 3.0, and most people would likely conclude that the higher estimate is more accurate.

This general approach can be extended to adjust for numerous known differences between the characteristics of the responding sample and the characteristics of the population to which we want to generalize our statistics. As the number of variables grows, the adjustments can get complicated, but computers can handle these complexities.

Interestingly, all analysts do not recommend using weighting to adjust for differences between known characteristics of the sampled population and the responding sample. The reason is a critical assumption, which is almost always untestable: that those responding from a particular subgroup are about the same as those not responding on the variables the survey is trying to estimate. In the example above, the assumption is that the males who did not respond would have reported a number of drinks similar to the reports of those who responded. What if the males who did not respond were disproportionately opposed to drinking alcohol? What if, in fact, the male nonrespondents not only actually drank less than the males who responded but, indeed, drank less than the females who responded. In that event, our nonresponse adjustment would have made our estimate worse, not better.

Many survey organizations routinely adjust their sample data by weighting to make the demographic (and sometimes other) composition correspond to known characteristics of the population they are trying to describe. To the extent that there is no association between characteristics they are adjusting and the variables they are trying to estimate, this weighting will have no effect on the resulting estimates. To the extent that there are relationships between the variables being estimated and the characteristics being adjusted, potentially there will be improvement in the estimates, *assuming that the nonrespondents in the adjusted groups are similar to respondents with respect to the variables being estimated.* However, if the nonrespondents are quite different, then these adjustments might make the estimates worse than if the sample data were left unweighted. Unless there is knowledge about these relationships, there is not a clear right answer about whether or not weighting to adjust for nonresponse in fact reduces survey error. Weighting a sample to make it mirror some known demographic characteristics of the population as a whole provides no real assurance by itself that the accuracy of other estimates based on the sample have been improved.

COPING WITH ITEM NONRESPONSE

In addition to the fact that some individuals selected to be in a sample do not provide any data at all, essentially all surveys have to deal with the fact that those responding to a survey do not provide codable answers to every question. There are two options: one can either leave those respondents who do not provide information out of an analysis, or one can try to estimate the answers they would have given if they had provided answers.

For most well-designed surveys, the rates of item nonresponse (items for which there are not values) are typically low. When item nonresponse is less than, say, 5%, the potential for that nonresponse to distort the estimates is fairly minimal. If a mean or other statistic is reported based only on those answering an item, the result is essentially assuming that the answers of item nonrespondents are the same as those responding. The true answers for nonrespondents have to be very divergent from those answering the questions to affect the distributions when they are fewer than 5%.

As the rate of item nonresponse rises, so does the potential for it to affect estimates. One way that leaving the item nonresponses out of an analysis affects the results is by reducing the number of observations on which a correlation or regression analysis is based. For this reason, many analytic packages will substitute the average answer for the whole sample for a nonresponse in order to include all respondents in an analysis. A more complicated and sophisticated approach, sometimes referred to as "imputation," is to build a model to predict the most likely answer for each respondent who does not answer a question. To do this, a researcher uses the data for those who answered a question to identify other survey questions that are good predictors of the question at issue. The predictive equation that results is then used to assign a value to those who did not answer the question.

This approach only improves the data to the extent that the model is a good predictor of the answers; it is obviously more complicated than leaving out the item nonrespondents, and it does not have much effect on analytic results when item nonresponse is low. On the other hand, when item response is high, there is considerable potential to improve estimates through imputation.

It is not uncommon to find that different imputation models produce different results. It is usually best to compare the results from several different models. If they produce similar results, then one can be reassured that the imputed estimates are likely to be improvements over assuming item nonrespondents would have given "average" answers. If the models produce quite different results, it is important to understand the reasons for the differences before deciding to use a particular approach for imputation.

Like any adjustment procedure, imputation has the potential to be misused and create more error than it reduces. However, when the models are good and item nonresponse is high, properly done imputations for missing data can make a positive contribution to data analyses.

ADJUSTING FOR DIFFERENT
PROBABILITIES OF SELECTION

As described in Chapter 3, many sample designs call for selecting certain individuals at higher rates than others. One of the most common reasons is the general policy of selecting only one respondent from a household. If households are selected, and one person is asked to respond, it means that adults living in households that contain three adults will be the respondent only one time in three, whereas adults living in a one-adult household will always be selected to be the respondents. Thus, the latter has three times the chance of selection as the former.

In other cases, samplers purposely try to sample some subgroups of a population at a higher than average rate to increase the ability to make reliable estimates of the characteristics of that subgroup.

Whenever there are differences in probabilities of selection, it is always appropriate to weight the responses so that *the weight times the probability of selection is the same for all respondents.*

Example: In a household sample, one adult per household is chosen to be the respondent. In order to adjust for the differences in probabilities of selection, responses are all weighted by the number of eligible adults in each household. Thus:

> If there is one adult, the probability of selection within the household is $1/1$ and the weight = 1
>
> If there are two adults, the probability of selection within the household is $1/2$ and the weight = 2
>
> If there are three adults, the probability of selection within the household is $1/3$ and the weight = 3
>
> If there are four adults, the probability of selection with the household is $1/4$, and the weight = 4

It is easy to see that the probability of selection times the weight is a constant = 1, no matter how many adults are in the household.

This same approach applies to any situation in which specific, identifiable subgroups of a population have different probabilities of selection. By weighting so that the probability of selection times the weight is the same for all respondents, these subgroups will be represented in the sample data in a way that should mirror their representation in the population from which the sample was drawn.

CALCULATING SAMPLING ERRORS

One of the strong reasons for using a probability sampling method is that it provides the basis for estimating sampling errors and calculating other statistics about the likely relationship between sample estimates and the characteristics of the population. If a sample was drawn as a simple random sample, with no clustering, no stratification, and equal probabilities of selection for all sample members, the calculation of standard errors is quite straightforward and can be done using almost any statistical package or even using the formulae and tables in Chapter 3. In the more common situation, when some deviation from simple random sampling is employed and some kind of weighting is required as part of the analysis, the statistical analysis needs to take into account those design features. If a program is used that does not appropriately adjust for the design, the estimates of sampling errors and calculation of statistical tests will be wrong.

Specifically, if weights are used to adjust for different probabilities of selection to correct for underrepresentation of some group or groups in the data, the number of observations on which calculations are based is likely to be distorted. Statistical tests critically depend on an estimate of the effective number of observations being analyzed.

Clustering in a sample usually increases the estimates of sampling errors, because clustering is likely to reduce the "effective" number of observations. Stratification of a sample usually reduces the estimates of standards errors, because stratification is likely to reduce uncontrolled variation in the composition of the sample. The huge challenge is that the effects of weighting, clustering, and stratification are not the same for all variables. Depending on how the values of a variable are in fact distributed with respect to the clusters, the strata, and the weights being used, the effects of appropriate adjustments will differ.

Fortunately, there are several widely available statistical packages that have the capability to make the appropriate adjustments to reflect the realities of the sample design. It is beyond the scope of this book to explicate the details of how those calculations are made. However, it is the task of the book to make it clear to readers that the details of the sample design and needed weighting do affect statistical tests, and that appropriate strategies must be incorporated into the analyses in order to correctly calculate standard errors and statistical significance.

CONCLUSION

Most of this book is devoted to the details of how to collect survey data in a way that maximizes their value for addressing analysis questions. It is beyond the scope of this book to cover analytic techniques and the related statistical issues. The issues addressed in this chapter, however, are directly related to the design and execution of a survey. As one makes inevitable tradeoffs about how data are to be collected, it is important to be thinking about how the data will be analyzed and to plan for appropriate adjustments in the analysis for the design decisions that are made and the virtually inevitable imperfections in the data that are collected.

Further Readings

Groves, R. M., Fowler, F. J., Couper, M. F., Lepkowski, J. M., Singer, E., & Tourangeau, R. (2004). *Survey methodology* (Chap. 10). New York: John Wiley.

11

Ethical Issues in Survey Research

Like all social research, surveys should be carried out in ways designed to avoid risks to participants, respondents, and interviewers. This chapter summarizes procedures for ethically managing surveys.

Like all research that involves human subjects, the survey researcher needs to be attentive to the ethical manner in which the research is carried out. A basic guideline is that the researcher should make sure that no individual suffers any adverse consequences as a result of the survey. Moreover, to the extent that it is feasible, a good researcher also will be attentive to maximizing positive outcomes of the research process. The foundation for most of the guidelines for protecting human subjects in research in the United States is the Belmont Report (National Commission for the Protection of Human Subjects, 1979).

Almost all universities and most other organizations in the United States that conduct federally funded research have an Institutional Review Board (IRB) that is responsible for overseeing research involving human subjects. When research is proposed, the Principal Investigator must submit the proposed protocol for IRB review before beginning to collect data.

IRB review is designed to protect subjects, researchers, and institutions. In general, the board's greatest concerns are about research that involves some kind of risk to participants. "Research activities in which the only involvement of human subjects will be . . . educational tests, survey procedures, or observation of public behavior . . . [are] exempt" unless:

1. information is recorded in such a way that human subjects can be identified. . . . **and**

2. any disclosure of the human subjects responses. . . . could reasonably place subjects at risk of criminal or civil liability or be damaging to the subjects' financial standing, employability, or reputation. (Department of Health and Human Services, 2005, p. 5)

Under these guidelines, many, if not most, surveys are technically exempt. That means that there is no basis for the IRB to scrutinize the details of the research or to recommend changes. However, because they involve subjects, material must be provided to the IRB so that someone (often the Chair) can determine that the protocol meets those standards. If the survey does involve some level of potential risk, or if vulnerable populations are involved, the IRB has the responsibility formally to review all procedures to make sure the human subjects are well protected.

In this text, it is not possible to address all the issues that may be involved in studies of special populations. Research on children, the mentally retarded, the mentally ill, prisoners, and other special populations may require attention for which researchers may get guidance elsewhere. Sieber (1992) provides much more detail on how to address data collection in an ethical way, as does a 2003 report from The National Academy of Sciences (Citro, Ilgen, & Marrett, 2003). The following, however, are some ethical principles about doing surveys of general populations with which all survey researchers should be familiar.

INFORMING RESPONDENTS

The survey research process generally involves enlisting voluntary cooperation. It is a basic premise of ethical survey research that respondents should be informed about what it is that they are volunteering for. Respondents should have the following information before being asked to answer questions:

1. The name of the organization that is carrying out the research. If an interviewer is involved, the respondent also should have the interviewer's name.

2. The sponsorship, that is, who is supporting or paying for the research.

3. A reasonably accurate, though brief, description of the purposes of the research. Is the research trying to increase general or basic knowledge, or is there some planning or action process that the research is designed to assist? What issues or topics is the research designed to cover? What questions is the research designed to address?

4. An accurate statement of the extent to which answers are protected with respect to confidentiality. If there are risks to or limits on the confidentiality that is being offered, they should be stated clearly.

5. Assurance that cooperation is voluntary and that no negative consequences will result for those who decide not to participate in the survey study.

6. Assurance that respondents can skip any questions that they do not want to answer.

This information may be mailed in advance or given directly to respondents, if the design permits. Regardless of what else is done, though, interviewers (if they are used) should be required to review the above points with respondents before beginning an interview.

Finally, perhaps a word is appropriate about signed consent forms. Generally speaking, respondents to sample surveys are not asked to sign forms prior to completing an interview. Obviously, it is not feasible to obtain signed forms on telephone surveys. Even in personal interview surveys, however, most thoughtful review committees feel that signed consent forms are not needed. In most cases, the risks involved in participation in surveys are quite minimal and well under the control of the respondent. In addition, respondents have an opportunity to re-exercise their decision to participate in a survey every time a new question is asked.

There are some exceptions. A signed form provides evidence that the researchers and their institutions in fact exposed respondents to certain key facts and that respondents agreed to the terms of the research. Researchers and Institutional Review Boards (IRBs) are more likely to want written documentation that respondents were fully informed when

1. Particularly sensitive information is collected that could, in fact, embarrass or harm someone if it became public.

2. There are important limits to the confidentiality of the data.

3. The population may lack the judgment or power to decline participation (e.g., children, prisoners, employees, students).

4. Access to information previously collected for some nonresearch purpose, such as medical records, is being sought in addition to survey answers.

These cases are the exception, not the rule. Most survey interviews do not require signed consent forms—only protocols that ensure that respondents are informed before they agree to participate. Again, Sieber (1992) discusses consent forms well.

PROTECTING RESPONDENTS

If a sample is drawn from a list, such as members of an insurance plan or employees of an organization, one very basic tenet of ethical research is that sample members' lives should not be adversely affected in any way by whether or not they agree to participate. To that end, whether or not people respond should not be shared with anyone outside the research team, and, when it is potentially an issue, sample persons should be assured that there will be no adverse results (e.g., on their health benefits, services, work situations, or grades) if they choose not to participate.

Beyond that, the main issue with respect to protecting survey respondents is the way in which the information they provide will be treated. Maintaining confidentiality in general is easier when answers are entered directly into a computer than when there is a paper questionnaire or interview schedule. Some standard procedures that careful survey researchers take to minimize the chances of a breach of confidentiality are as follows:

- All people who have access to the data or a role in the data collection are committed in writing to confidentiality.

- Links between answers and identifiers are minimized. Names, e-mail or postal addresses, and telephone numbers are the most common identifiers. Often names are not required in order to execute a proper survey; when they can be avoided, many survey organizations do not use names in any part of the research process.

- When there are specific identifiers such as names, addresses, or telephone numbers, they are put in a form that can be readily separated from the actual survey responses. Identifiers (other than a coded id number) should be physically removed from completed survey instruments as soon as possible.

- If names or addresses were used to identify the sample or collect data, those names and addresses are deleted or destroyed once they are no longer needed.

- Completed survey returns are not accessible to nonproject members. If they are in paper form, keeping them in locked files is preferred.

- Individuals who could identify respondents from their profile of answers (e.g., supervisors in the case of a survey of employees, or teachers in the case of a survey of students) are not permitted to see the actual survey responses.

- The actual data files usually will have some kind of an ID number for each respondent. The link between the ID number and the sample addresses or the identifiers is not available to general users of the data file.

- During analysis, researchers are careful about presenting data for very small categories of people who might be identifiable.

- When a project is completed, or when use of the actual survey instruments is over, it is the responsibility of the researcher to see to the eventual destruction of completed survey research instruments, or their continuing secure storage.

Obviously, deviation from these particular procedures may be required for a given project. The general approach and concerns reflected in this set of procedures, however, should typify any responsible survey research project. One low probability but important possible limit to promised confidentiality of survey data is that questionnaires and records can be subpoenaed by a court. Researchers can protect themselves from this threat to promised confidentiality in several ways. If research involves especially sensitive material, such as drug or criminal justice studies might entail, researchers can petition federal or state agencies for a certificate of confidentiality that provides protection from subpoena. Alternatively, concerned researchers can destroy the link, before any subpoena is issued, between identifiers and responses so that it is impossible to associate respondents with their answers. If maintaining the link is essential, as in the case of a longitudinal study that entails repeated contact with respondents, researchers have been known to send the file linking individuals and responses to another country, out of the jurisdiction of U.S. courts. Again, Sieber (1992) is a good source for more detail on these issues.

BENEFITS TO RESPONDENTS

In most surveys, the main benefits to respondents are intrinsic: enjoying the process of the interview or feeling they contributed to a worthwhile effort. More direct benefits, such as payment, prizes, or services, are sometimes provided. When services are offered, attention must be paid to providing them in a way that does not compromise the promised confidentiality of the survey answers. Also, as the use of cash incentives to participate becomes more common, concern has been raised that incentives should not be so large that it becomes unreasonably difficult for some respondents, particularly those in financial distress, to say "no." Benefits should not be so great as to undermine the principle that research participation is a voluntary act. Other than that, the key ethical responsibility is to be certain not to overstate the benefits and to deliver the benefits promised. In particular, the researcher who enlists cooperation by describing the uses of the research assumes a commitment to ensure appropriate analysis and dissemination of the data.

ETHICAL RESPONSIBILITIES TO INTERVIEWERS

Beyond the obligations of any employer, the researcher has responsibilities to interviewers in two areas. First, the interviewer is given the responsibility of presenting the research to the respondents. It is the researcher's obligation to make sure that interviewers have full and accurate information to give about the research. The researcher should not put the interviewer in a position of being deceptive, misleading, or inaccurate.

Second, the researcher must deal with interviewer safety and fear of crime. Because general household samples will include all areas, interviewers may have to visit neighborhoods in which they do not feel safe. The following guidelines may be helpful:

• Interviewers legitimately can be asked to visit sample addresses in a car before deciding they do not feel safe. Neighborhood areas are heterogeneous and vary from block to block.

• Interviewers should be told explicitly that it is not a job requirement to go somewhere under circumstances that they feel are unsafe. Options include avoiding night calls, using weekend days to interview employed people, and interviewing with another interviewer or a paid escort. A good approach is to ask interviewers to work with the field supervisor to figure out how to carry out interviews in a way that feels safe.

• Interviewers should be briefed on sensible procedures to reduce the risks of their being victims.

Fortunately, victimization is rare; fear is more the problem. In our society, however, crimes do occur. Both researchers and interviewers need to feel that interviewers were informed and were not pressured to go anywhere or to do anything that would increase the real likelihood that they would be a victim of a crime.

CONCLUSION

The ethical issues in survey research are not different from those in the social sciences in general. The real risks and potential costs of being a respondent (or interviewer) in most surveys are minimal. Certain basic steps, though, are needed to reduce whatever risks there are either to participants or to the image of social science researchers. The specific steps outlined above are by no means exhaustive. The basic approach of dealing with everyone in an honest way, however, with continuing attention to the details that will maximize benefits and avoid costs, should be an integral part of any survey research effort.

Further Readings

Citro, C., Ilgen, D., & Marrett, C. (2003). *Protecting participants and facilitating social and behavioral sciences research.* Washington, DC: National Academy Press.

Groves, R. M., Fowler, F. J., Couper, M. P., Lepkowski, J. M., Singer, E., & Tourangeau, R. (2004). *Survey methodology* (Chap. 11). New York: John Wiley.

Sieber, J. (1992). *Planning ethically responsible research: Developing an effective protocol.* Newbury Park, CA: Sage.

12

Providing Information About Survey Methods

Researchers reporting survey estimates have a scientific obligation to provide a full description of the details of the procedures they used that could affect those estimates. In addition, they should perform and report calculations relevant to the precision and accuracy of their figures. This chapter discusses the material that should be included in a full methodological description of a survey.

There are few methodological decisions that a researcher could make that could be labeled categorically as wrong. There are some research situations in which any of the compromises discussed in this book might be appropriate and cost effective for gathering information. Although research design decisions cannot be criticized out of context, the failure to fully describe procedures by which data were collected can be criticized. It is essential for readers and users of survey data to have access to a full and complete description of the data collection process.

There are two general functions of a good methodological description. The first is to provide a good understanding of how well sample estimates are likely to describe the population from which the sample was drawn. It is not enough simply to state the author's conclusions on this matter; detailed calculations relevant to precision and bias should be presented that will permit readers to make their own assessments. The second function is to provide the procedural details needed to replicate a data collection effort and/or detect procedural differences between surveys that would affect comparability.

It is not unusual to find only the sample size reported about a survey; more conscientious researchers will include a description of their sampling strategies and response rates. Although the appropriate level of detail will vary with the way the data are being used, the following is a brief outline of information that should be provided about any survey.

- The sample frame (i.e., those people from whom the sample was drawn), together with an estimate of the percentage of the population studied that had a chance of selection from that frame and anything that is known about the way in which the excluded people differ from the population as a whole.

• The sampling procedure, including any deviations from simple random sampling such as clustering, stratification, or unequal rates of selection among subgroups of the population.

• Field results, the disposition of the initially designated sample: the number of respondents, the number of nonrespondents, and the major reasons for nonresponse. If the rate of response cannot be calculated exactly because the sample frame included ineligible units (e.g., telephone numbers not associated with occupied housing units), the researcher should report the number of units for which eligibility was not ascertained and an estimate of the most likely response rate. The American Association of Public Opinion Research has published a good monograph on the reporting of response rates to improve the consistency of reporting and the terminology that researchers use when reporting their results (AAPOR, 2006).

• The exact wording of questions analyzed. For a major report, the entire survey instrument should be reproduced in an appendix.

In addition to factual description of the data collection process, there are five other desiderata in a methodological appendix.

First, most reports are intended for audiences that go beyond survey research methodologists. Therefore, a brief overview of the possible kinds of error in surveys usually is an appropriate introduction to a methodological section of a survey.

Second, numerical estimates of the amount of sampling error associated with the particular design of the sample should be included. If the sample design was stratified and clustered, or if different rates of selection were used, the effects of those design features will be different for different measures in the survey. Typically, researchers calculate these design effects for a number of measures in the survey, including some they expect to be most and least affected by the sample design. They then either present the design effects for these items or report the range of the design effects, with some generalizations about the kinds of items that are affected most by the sample design.

Third, if interviewers are used, information about interviewers relevant to their likely effects on the data is desirable. A minimum description would be the number of interviewers who collected data, how much training interviewers received, and whether or not a sample of their work was monitored. Age, gender, and ethnicity of interviewers are useful to know if those characteristics are relevant to the survey content.

As discussed in Chapter 8, interviewer effects cannot be calculated reliably if respondents are assigned to interviewers on the basis of convenience. There is a growing body of data on the size of interviewer effects, however, summarized by

Groves (1989), which can be used to tell readers about the likely range of interviewer effects on estimates. In addition, telephone surveys from central facilities make it possible to manage interviewer assignments so that reasonable estimates of interviewer effects can be made. It would be desirable if more studies were done so that interviewer effects could be estimated, and if the resulting estimates became a common feature of methodological reports of surveys.

Fourth, a researcher should tell readers as much as is known about the effect of nonresponse on sample estimates. This requirement is particularly important when response rates for a survey are comparatively low. If the researcher sampled from a source that provides information about those from whom responses were not obtained, that information should be presented. Interviewers should be encouraged to get at least some information about people who refuse so the researcher can say something about ways in which nonrespondents may differ from respondents. If there are statistics from other sources about the population from which the sample was drawn, such as relatively recent census figures, the researcher can compare the sample with such independent aggregate figures to estimate some effects of nonresponse on the sample. Usually, there are no data about how nonresponse is related to the key measures in a survey. However, whatever data can be presented about nonrespondents will help readers evaluate how nonresponse error may affect results.

Finally, a good methodological appendix should include some information about the reliability and validity of the major measures used in a survey. There are three kinds of relevant information that can be reported.

First, if questions were subjected to cognitive laboratory testing or systematic pretesting, that fact and the results can be reported. Simply reporting the kind of question evaluation that was done can be useful to users of the results. It is valuable to be told that questions were found to be comprehensible and that coding of behavior during pretests revealed that questions were asked as worded and usually could be answered readily. Also, sometimes pretesting indicates a problem with a question that, nonetheless, is retained. Such information obviously is also very helpful to users of the resulting data.

Second, researchers can present analyses that assess the validity of the question answers. To the extent that answers correlate in predictable ways with the answers to other questions, there is evidence that they are measuring what the researcher was hoping to measure. Ware (1987) presents a good outline of the kinds of analyses that a thorough assessment of reliability and validity should entail.

Third, although the accuracy of reporting of factual data seldom can be assessed directly in a survey, citing the results of record-check studies of the reporting of similar items can provide readers with one basis for estimating the amount and direction of error in a survey-based estimate.

To date there has been a relative dearth of systematic data about how well questions measure what they are intended to measure. It probably is fair to say that the majority of survey reports assume face validity, that answers mean what the designer of the question thought they would mean. It would be desirable if the collection of data and analyses directed at assessing questions and answers, and making reports of question assessment, became a more routine part of reports of survey methodology.

There will be reports of survey data for which all the information outlined above would be too detailed. There is always pressure to shorten journal articles. All of the information, however, is decidedly relevant to the assessment of the likely quality of a survey-based estimate. In a full report of a survey analysis, a full methodological appendix should be included. When shorter works are published, a methodological report covering the details of the data collection process at least should be available on request.

It should be noted, in conclusion, that the list of desiderata is as much about the importance of gathering and analyzing information about measurement as it is about reporting it. It obviously is desirable to take steps to minimize error, but error-free surveys are not possible. Documenting how well the measurement was done, and estimating the amount and type of error in the results, is a critical part of ensuring appropriate use of survey data. It also is an important part of constructing the knowledge base on which to build better survey measurement in the future.

Therefore, when survey results are reported, there is an obligation to report the information needed to assess the quality of the data, as well as to replicate the results. The latter goal can be achieved by carefully describing the procedures used; the former goal requires special effort to measure error as well as to communicate the results. When a report is silent about some kind of error, such as whether questions are intelligible or whether interviewers affected the results, the implicit assumption made by most readers is that there is no problem. At the least, researchers can make sure readers know about the various sources of error that can affect survey estimates (desideratum number 1). In the longer run, however, it is to be hoped that the steps required to provide specific estimates of error will become increasingly routine in reporting survey results.

EXERCISE

Using the standards presented in this chapter, systematically evaluate the adequacy and completeness of the methodological section of a published book or report that was based on a survey.

13

Survey Error in Perspective

Total survey design involves considering all aspects of a survey and choosing a level of rigor appropriate to the particular project purposes. The most common deviations from good survey design and practice are discussed in this chapter, together with an assessment of their cost-saving potential and their significance for the precision, accuracy, and credibility of survey estimates.

THE CONCEPT OF TOTAL SURVEY DESIGN

Total survey design means that when designing a survey or evaluating the quality of survey data, one looks at the complete data collection process, not simply at one or two aspects of the survey. The quality of the sample (the frame, the size, the design, and the response rate), the quality of the questions as measures, the quality of data collection (especially the use of effective interviewer training and supervising procedures), and the mode of data collection constitute a tightly interrelated set of issues and design decisions, all with the potential to affect the quality of the resulting survey data. The full appreciation of the total survey design approach to survey error has three concrete implications:

1. In designing a survey data collection, the researcher self-consciously takes into account trade-offs between costs and methodological rigor in all aspects of the survey design process. Investments in error reduction in one aspect of the survey are not made when other aspects of the survey do not warrant that level of investment.

2. In evaluating the quality of data, researchers ask questions about how all of the decisions affecting data quality were made and carried out.

3. In reporting the details of a survey, a researcher will report relevant details of all aspects of the data collection effort that impinge on the error level of the data.

ERROR IN PERSPECTIVE

It is difficult to generalize across all projects regarding the significance of the various methodological choices discussed in this book. The cost of making the rigorous decision varies a great deal across choices as well as varying from research situation to situation. In the same way, the potential for error from making the less costly decision also varies greatly. The notion of a custom design for a survey means that a researcher should go down the list of design options carefully, assess the alternatives, assess the cost and potential for error, and make decisions about which compromises make sense and which do not. The following are some possible generalizations, however, that may be helpful.

It is fairly rare to have a perfect sample frame that gives every member of the population that the researcher wants to study a known chance of selection. Whom to sample truly is a decision that cannot be evaluated out of context. It is incumbent on researchers, though, to be very clear about how comprehensive their sample frame was and who was omitted, and not to imply that their sample estimates apply to people who had no chance to be sampled.

Probably the most common cost-saving compromises in survey research occur in the sampling area. At worst, people try to generalize from data collected from people who were not sampled at all, such as magazine readers or Internet users who voluntarily fill out questionnaires. Using nonprobability samples, however, substituting more available or willing people for those more difficult to enlist in a sample, is a common practice; it is typical of many public opinion, political, and market research polls. In fact, for telephone surveys, permitting sample substitution does not save a great deal of money, though it does permit doing surveys quickly. For household interviews in person, however, there is a considerable cost difference between probability and nonprobability samples. The major price one pays for such cost savings is to give up statistical credibility with respect to the error in the data; there is no scientific basis for describing the relationship of the sample to the population sampled. If the goal of a survey is to solicit the views of a broader spectrum of the population than would be readily at hand in some other way, such nonstatistical sampling procedures may serve the purpose well. Nevertheless, if more than order of magnitude estimates are of interest and when scientific credibility is an issue, the cost savings derived from sample substitution probably are not worth it.

An almost equally common compromise in surveys is to accept low response rates. Almost all studies of early returns of mail questionnaires show that they are a biased sample, biased in ways that are relevant directly to the subject matter of the survey. The biases associated with low response rates to telephone surveys are somewhat less dramatic. The real problem is that we lack good information about when nonresponse is likely to seriously affect estimates. Error due to nonresponse is common and often large, but the amount of error is not highly correlated with the response rate (Groves, 2006). That makes it hard to say when a response rate is too low and when significant additional effort is essential. The bottom line is credibility. Data based on low response rates are easy to criticize, and researchers have to decide how much that matters.

Because most people who think about survey design think about sampling, very little time will be spent here on that topic. If one is going to draw a sophisticated sample, the help of a qualified sampling statistician is needed. Presumably, such a statistician will consider trade-offs among various sampling schemes for the calculation of sampling errors. The one point that should be noted here is that the majority of population samples involve some clustering. In fact, multistage clustered samples are the best solution to a wide range of sampling problems. It is not uncommon, however, to see reports in which the effects of clustering are ignored in estimates of sampling error. If researchers do not have an effective simple random sample, which is often the case, they cannot use simple random sampling assumptions in estimating standard errors.

The choice of data collection mode is one of the most fundamental choices affecting survey costs. Though for years personal survey methods were considered the only effective way to carry out general population surveys, telephone strategies are now far more prevalent than personal interview surveys in most survey organizations.

For many purposes, the telephone has proved an effective way to produce survey data. Depending on the situation, telephone interviewing may be at a disadvantage in leaving out the segment of the population without landline telephones (the sample frame problem), in producing higher rates of nonresponse (although this is not always the case), and in permitting researchers to collect less data (because telephone interviews generally are designed to run shorter than personal interviews). Telephone survey procedures are the right answer for many projects. As with most cost-saving procedures, though, there are occasions when the nonmonetary price for choosing the telephone is too high.

Mail and Internet data collection protocols clearly are attractive ways to collect information from some populations. Their comparatively low costs also make them strong candidates for use in combination with more costly methods. The less expensive methods can be used to collect data from those who will use these modes, while other approaches can be used to collect data from those who are less motivated to respond or who cannot respond easily to some mode (for example, because they lack Internet access). Figuring out how to match mode of data collection to the sample, subject matter, and instrument requirements in a way that is cost effective and will produce good response rates is one of the most essential elements of a good survey design. Alternatively, relying solely on a mode that is inappropriate or ineffective for some part of the study population is a clear example of poor survey design.

The quality of the interviewing staff is one of the least appreciated aspects of survey research. It has been shown that good training and supervision have significant effects on how interviewers conduct interviews. Also, for a good number of common survey questions, poorly trained or supervised interviewers can increase the margin of error around estimates, just as having a smaller sample might do. This means that when there are important interviewer effects on answers, a sample of 1,000 may have the effective precision of a sample of only 700. Although the significance of interviewing quality varies with the content of the survey and the kinds of questions, most general-purpose surveys will have at least some questions that will be affected significantly by interviewers. In this context, skimping on interviewer training and supervision may be a poor choice.

The quality of the interviewing staff also affects the response rate. Using a good interviewing staff that has proven it can achieve respondent cooperation is one of the easiest ways to ensure a good response rate. Close supervision, retraining, and the elimination of interviewers who are not good at enlisting cooperation are also steps that will pay off in reduced nonresponse and probably will not entail much extra cost.

Standardized procedures that structure the way that interviewers explain the interview task to respondents can be built into surveys. Such techniques have been shown to be a virtually cost-free way to improve the average level of respondent performance.

Finally, thorough evaluation of survey questions may be one of the most important and cost-effective ways to reduce survey error. Through appropriate use of focus groups and cognitive interviews, researchers can improve the degree to which questions are understood consistently and answered validly. Systematic studies of behavior in field pretests can identify questions that interviewers do not ask in a consistent way or that pose problems for respondents. Improving questions can both improve the validity of respondent reporting and reduce the effect of interviewers on answers.

CONCLUSION

The goals of good design and practice are to produce the most accuracy, credibility, and replicability possible for each dollar. How precise, credible, and replicable a particular study should be depends on the problem to be addressed and how the information will be used.

One will occasionally read that social science is inexact, and invidious comparisons are made between the measurement processes in the social sciences and those in physical sciences. Although such conclusions are common, they commonly are uninformed. Basic measurements in physical and biomedical sciences, such as the level of lead in a blood sample, the readings of blood pressures, reading of X-rays, and the measures of the elasticity of metals, all prove to have nontrivial levels of unreliability. Measurement in any of these fields can be made either better or worse by the methodology used and the care that goes into the design of the measurement process; Turner and Martin (1984) provide numerous examples. The same is true for survey research.

Minimizing error in surveys usually comes at a cost. In some cases, the value of the best measurement possible is not worth the cost. Sampling a population by sampling households omits people who cannot be associated with households. This is a very small fraction of the total population in most areas, however, and the cost of finding a way to sample people who cannot be associated with households is extraordinary.

Nonresponse rates can be reduced to virtually zero. The Bureau of the Census routinely achieves response rates in excess of 90% for the National Health Interview Survey and the Current Population Survey, though response rates are lower in some major central cities. If one wanted to spend enough time and money, one could probably achieve response rates close to 100% even in the most inhospitable segments of our most difficult central cities. Again, however, the cost would be extraordinary, and the potential error reduction modest.

Fortunately, respondents are able and willing to answer many questions of great interest to social scientists and policymakers. For some other questions, it would be convenient if respondents were able and willing to answer in a standard survey process, but they are not. For example, drunk driving convictions and bankruptcies are underreported markedly using standard survey techniques (Locander et al., 1976). There probably is some way that a research project could be presented that would induce most people to report such facts accurately, but it would take a great deal more effort than researchers generally make to gain respondent cooperation. Again there are decisions to be made about how much accuracy and detail are worth in the context of how the data will be used. Readers are referred to Groves (1989) for a much more extensive analysis of the relationship between survey costs and survey error.

It has been said that the limit of survey research is what people are able and willing to tell us in the context of the survey. Those limits, however, can be stretched. There certainly are some real limits to what can be measured accurately using standardized survey procedures. Even so, the limits probably are related much more often to budgetary considerations and how much effort the researcher wants to put into the measurement process than to what is actually feasible.

The context in which one evaluates a design is whether or not the compromises made were the right ones, the intelligent ones, and the ones that would produce data appropriate to the purposes at hand. It also is worth pointing out that survey error does not result solely from thoughtful, cost-saving decisions. There also has not been adequate appreciation of the significance of nonresponse, question design, and interviewer performance for the quality of survey estimates. Sheer lack of attention to these important aspects of data collection routinely produces survey data that lack credibility or do not meet state-of-the-art standards for reliability.

Appreciating the concept of total design articulated in this book should mean the following:

• No feature of a data collection will be so poor or so weak that it would undermine the researcher's ability to use the data to achieve the survey's goals.

• The design of all phases of the data collection will be relatively consistent, so that investments are not made in producing precision in one aspect of the data collection process that are not justified by the level of precision that other aspects of the design will generate.

• Users of survey data will have an appropriate respect for the uses of the estimates based on a sample survey, the likely sources of error in surveys, and the limits in accuracy and confidence that they can have in survey-based estimates.

Finally, it is hoped that users of research will have a thorough grasp of the questions they should ask about the data collection in any survey, that researchers have a better grasp of the significance of the details of the design decisions, and that all readers come away with a renewed commitment to better survey design and execution.

References

American Association for Public Opinion Research. (2006). *Standard definitions: Final dispositions of case codes and outcome rates for surveys* (4th ed.). Lenexa, KS: AAPOR.

Anderson, B., Silver, B., & Abramson, P. (1988). The effects of race of the interviewer on measures of electoral participation by blacks. *Public Opinion Quarterly, 52*(1), 53–83.

Aquilino, W. S. (1994). Interview mode effects in surveys of drug and alcohol use: A field experiment. *Public Opinion Quarterly, 58*(2), 210–240.

Aquilino, W. S. (1998). Effects of interview mode on measuring depression in younger adults. *Journal of Official Statistics, 14*(1), 15–30.

Aquilino, W. S., & Losciuto, L. A. (1990). Effects of mode of interview on self-reported drug use. *Public Opinion Quarterly, 54*(3), 362–391.

Baker, R. P., Crawford, S., & Swinehart, J. (2004). Development and testing of Web questionnaires. In S. Presser et al. (Eds.), *Methods for testing and evaluating survey questionnaires* (pp. 361–384). New York: John Wiley.

Beatty, P. (1995). Understanding the standardized/non-standardized interviewing controversy, *Journal of Official Statistics, 11*(2), 147–160.

Belli, R. F., Lee, E. H., Stafford, F. P., & Chou, C. (2004). Calendar and question-list survey methods: Association between interviewer behaviors and data quality. *Journal of Official Statistics, 20*(2), 185–218.

Belson, W. A. (1981). *The design and understanding of survey questions.* Aldershot, UK: Gower.

Berry, S., & Kanouse, D. (1987). Physician response to a mailed survey: An experiment in timing of payment. *Public Opinion Quarterly, 51*(1), 102–114.

Billiet, J., & Loosveldt, G. (1988). Interviewer training and quality of responses. *Public Opinion Quarterly, 52*(2), 190–211.

Bishop, G. F., Hippler, H. J., Schwartz, N., & Strack, F. (1988). A comparison of response effects in self-administered and telephone surveys. In R. M. Groves, P. N. Biemer, L. E. Lyberg, J. T. Massey, W. L. Nichols II, & J. Waksberg (Eds.), *Telephone survey methodology* (pp. 321–340). New York: John Wiley.

Blom, E., & Lyberg, L. (1998). Scanning and optical character recognition in survey organizations. In M. P. Couper et al. (Eds.), *Computer assisted survey information collection* (pp. 449–520). New York: John Wiley.

Blumberg, S., Lake, J., & Cynamon, M. (2006). Telephone coverage and health survey estimates: Evaluating concerns about wireless substitutes. *American Journal of Public Health, 96*, 926–931.

Bradburn, N. M., & Sudman, S. (1992). The current status of questionnaire design. In P. N. Beimer, R. M. Groves, L. E. Lyberg, N. Mathiowetz, & S. Sudman (Eds.), *Measurement errors in surveys* (pp. 29–40). New York: John Wiley.

Bradburn, N. M., Sudman, S., & Associates (1979). *Improving interview method and questionnaire design.* San Francisco: Jossey-Bass.

Brick, J. M., Dipko, S., Presser, S., Tucker, C., & Yuan, Y. (2006). Nonresponse bias in a dual frame sample of cell and landline numbers. *Public Opinion Quarterly, 70*(5), 780–793.

Brick, J. M., Waksberg, J., Kulp, D., & Starer, A. (1995). Bias in list-assisted telephone samples. *Public Opinion Quarterly, 59,* 218–235.

Bryson, M. (1976, November). The Literary Digest poll: Making of a statistical myth. *American Statistician,* pp. 184–185.

Burton, S., & Blair, E. (1991). Task conditions, response formulation processes, and response accuracy for behavioral frequency questions in surveys. *Public Opinion Quarterly, 55,* 50–79.

Cannell, C., & Fowler, F. (1964). A note on interviewer effect in self-enumerative procedures. *American Sociological Review, 29,* 276.

Cannell, C., Groves, R., Magilavy, L., Mathiowetz, N., & Miller, P. (1987). An experimental comparison of telephone and personal health interview surveys. *Vital & Health Statistics,* Series 2, 106. Washington, DC: Government Printing Office.

Cannell, C., Marquis, K., & Laurent, A. (1977). A summary of studies. *Vital & Health Statistics,* Series 2, 69. Washington, DC: Government Printing Office.

Cannell, C., & Oksenberg, L. (1988). Observation of behaviour in telephone interviewers. In R. M. Groves, P. N. Biemer, L. E. Lyberg, J. T. Massey, W. L. Nichols II, & J. Waksberg (Eds.), *Telephone survey methodology* (pp. 475–495). New York: John Wiley.

Cannell, C., Oksenberg, L., & Converse, J. (1977). *Experiments in interviewing techniques: Field experiments in health reporting, 1971–1977.* Hyattsville, MD: National Center for Health Services Research.

Catania, J. A., Gibson, D., Chitwood, D., & Coates, T. (1990). Methodological problems in AIDS behavioral research: Influences on measurement error and participation bias in studies of sexual behavior. *Psychological Bulletin, 108*(3), 339–362.

Catlin, O., & Ingram, S. (1988). The effects of CATI on costs and data quality: A comparison of CATI and paper methods in centralized interviewing. In R. M. Groves, P. N., Biemer, L. E., Lyberg, J. T., Massey, W. L. Nichols II. & J. Waksberg (Eds.), *Telephone survey methodology* (pp. 437–445). New York: John Wiley.

Chromy, J. R., Eyerman, J., Odom, D., McNeeley, M. E., & Hughes, A. (2005). Association between interviewer experience and substance use prevalence rates in NSDUH. In J. Kennett & J. Gfoerrer (Eds.), *Evaluating and improving methods used in the NSDUH* (DHHS Publication number SMA 05-4044, methodology series M-5) (pp. 59–87). Rockville, MD: SAMSA.

Citro, C., Ilgen, D., & Marrett, C. (2003). *Protecting participants and facilitating social and behavioral sciences research.* Washington, DC: National Academy Press.

Conrad, F. G., & Schober, M. F. (2000). Clarifying question meaning in a household telephone survey. *Public Opinion Quarterly, 64*(1), 1–28.

Converse, J. (1987). *Survey research in the United States.* Berkeley: University of California Press.

Converse, J., & Presser, S. (1986). *Survey questions.* Beverly Hills, CA: Sage.

Couper, M. P. (2007). Issues of representation in eHealth research (with a focus on Web surveys). *American Journal of Preventive Medicine, 32*(5S), S83–S89.

Couper, M. P., et al. (Eds.). (1998). *Computer assisted survey information collection.* New York: John Wiley.

Couper, M. P., Hansen, S. E., & Sadowsky, S. A. (1997). Evaluating interviewer use of CAPI technology. In L. E. Lyberg, P. Beimer, M. Collins, & E. D. de Leeuw (Eds.), *Survey measurement and process quality* (pp. 267–286). New York: John Wiley.

Cronbach, L. (1951). Coefficient alpha and the internal structure of tests. *Psychiatrika, 16,* 297–334.

Cronbach, L., & Meehl, P. (1955). Construct validity in psychological tests. *Psychological Bulletin, 52,* 281–302.

de Leeuw, E. D. (2008). Choosing the method of data collection. In E. D. de Leeuw, J. J. Hox, & D. A. Dillman (Eds.), *International handbook of survey methodology* (pp. 113–135). Mahwah, NJ: Lawrence Erlbaum.

de Leeuw, E. D., & de Heer, W. (2002). Trends in household survey nonresponse: A longitudinal and international comparison. In R. M. Groves, D. A. Dillman, J. E. Eltinge, & R. J. A. Little (Eds.), *Survey nonresponse* (pp. 41–54). New York: John Wiley.

de Leeuw, E. D., Dillman, D. A., & Hox, J. J. (2008). Mixed mode surveys: When and why. In E. D. de Leeuw, J. J. Hox, & D. A. Dillman (Eds.), *International handbook of survey methodology* (pp. 299–316). Mahwah, NJ: Lawrence Erlbaum.

de Leeuw, E. D., & van der Zouwen, J. (1988). Data quality in telephone and face to face surveys: A comparative meta-analysis. In R. M. Groves, P. N. Biemer, L. E. Lyberg, J. T. Massey, W. L. Nichols II, & J. Waksberg (Eds.), *Telephone survey methodology* (pp. 283–299). New York: John Wiley.

DeMaio, T. J., & Rothgeb, J. M. (1996). Cognitive interviewing techniques—in the lab and in the field. In N. A. Schwarz & S. Sudman (Eds.), *Answering questions* (pp. 177–196). San Francisco: Jossey-Bass.

Department of Health and Human Services. (2005). *Protection of human subjects.* Title 45, Code of Regulations, Part 46. Washington, DC: Government Printing Office.

DeVellis, R. F. (2003). *Scale development: Theory and applications.* Newbury Park, CA: Sage.

Dielman, L., & Couper, M. P. (1995). Data quality in CAPI survey: Keying errors. *Journal of Official Statistics, 11*(2), 141–146.

Dillman, D. A. (2007). *Mail and Internet surveys: The tailored design method* (2nd ed.). New York: John Wiley.

Dillman, D. (2008). The logic and psychology of constructing questionnaires. In E. D. de Leeuw, J. J. Hox, & D. A. Dillman (Eds.), *International handbook of survey methodology* (pp. 161–175). Mahwah, NJ: Lawrence Erlbaum.

Dillman, D. A., & Miller, K. J. (1998). Response rates, data and feasibility for optical scannable mail surveys for small research centers. In M. P. Couper et al. (Eds.), *Computer assisted survey information collection* (pp. 475–498). New York: John Wiley.

Dillman, D. A., & Redline, C. D. (2004). Testing self-administered questionnaires: Cognitive interview and field test comparision. In S. Presser et al. (Eds.), *Methods for testing and evaluating survey questionnaires* (pp. 299–318). New York: John Wiley.

Dillman, D. A., & Tarnai, J. (1991). Mode effects of cognitively designed recall questions: A comparison of answers to telephone and mail surveys. In P. N. Biemer, R. M. Corres, L. E. Lyberg, N. A. Mathiowetz, & S. Sudman (Eds.), *Measurement errors in surveys* (pp. 367–393). New York: John Wiley.

Dykema, J., Lepkowski, J., & Blixt, S. (1997). The effect of interviewer and respondent behavior on data quality: Analysis of interaction coding in a validation study. In L. Lyberg et al. (Eds.), *Survey measurement and process quality* (pp. 287–310). New York: John Wiley.

Edwards, W. S., et al. (1994). Evaluation of National Health Interview Survey diagnostic reporting. In *Vital & Health Statistics,* Series 2, No. 120. Hyattville, MD: National Center for Health Statistics.

Edwards, W. S., Winn, D. M., & Collins, J. G. (1996). Evaluation of 2-week doctor visit reporting in the National Health Interview Survey. In *Vital & Health Statistics,* Series 2, No. 122. Hyattsville, MD: National Center for Health Statistics.

Erlich, J., & Riesman, D. (1961). Age and authority in the interview. *Public Opinion Quarterly, 24,* 99–114.

Filion, F. (1975). Estimating bias due to nonresponse in mail surveys. *Public Opinion Quarterly, 39*(4), 482–492.

Forsyth, B. H., & Lessler, J. T. (1992). Cognitive laboratory methods: A taxonomy. In P. N. Biemer, R. M. Groves, L. E. Lyberg, N. A. Mathiowetz, & S. Sudman (Eds.), *Measurement errors in surveys* (pp. 393–418). New York: John Wiley.

Fowler, F. J. (1991). Reducing interviewer related error through interviewer training, supervision, and other means. In P. N. Biemer, R. M. Groves, L. E. Lyberg, N. A. Mathiowetz, & S. Sudman (Eds.), *Measurement errors in surveys* (pp. 259–278). New York: John Wiley.

Fowler, F. J. (1992). How unclear terms affect survey data. *Public Opinion Quarterly, 56*(2), 218–231.

Fowler, F. J. (1995). *Improving survey questions.* Thousand Oaks, CA: Sage.

Fowler, F. J. (2004). Getting beyond pretesting and cognitive interviews: The case for more experimental pilot studies. In S. Presser et al. (Eds.), *Questionnaire development, evaluation, and testing methods* (pp. 173–188). New York: John Wiley.

Fowler, F. J., & Cannell, C. F. (1996). Using behavioral coding to identify cognitive problems with survey questions. In N. A. Schwarz & S. Sudman (Eds.), *Answering questions* (pp. 15–36). San Francisco: Jossey-Bass.

Fowler, F. J., & Cosenza, C. (2008). Writing effective survey questions. In J. Hox, E. D. de Leeuw, & D. Dillman (Eds.), *The international handbook of survey methodology* (pp. 136–160). Mahwah, NJ: Lawrence Erlbaum.

Fowler, F. J., Gallagher, P. M., Stringfellow, V. L., Zaslavsky, A. M., Thompson, J. W., & Cleary, P. D. (2002). Using telephone interviewers to reduce nonresponse bias to mail surveys of health plan members. *Medical Care, 40*(3), 190–200.

Fowler, F. J., & Mangione, T. W. (1990). *Standardized survey interviewing: Minimizing interviewer related error.* Newbury Park, CA: Sage.

Fowler, F. J., Roman, A. M., & Di, Z. X (1998). Mode effects in a survey of Medicare prostate surgery patients. *Public Opinion Quarterly, 62*(1), 29–46.

Fox, J. A., & Tracy, P. E. (1986). *Randomized response: A method for sensitive surveys.* Beverly Hills, CA: Sage.

Fox, R., Crask, M., & Kim, J. (1988). Mail survey response rate: A meta-analysis of selected techniques for increasing response. *Public Opinion Quarterly, 52*(4), 467–491.

Friedman, P. A. (1942). A second experiment in interviewer bias. *Sociometry, 15,* 378–381.

Gallagher, P. M., Fowler, F. J., & Stringfellow, V. (2005). The nature of nonresponse in a Medicaid survey: Causes and consequences. *Journal of Official Statistics, 21*(1), 73–87.

Graesser, A. C., Cai, Z., Louwerse, M., & Daniel, F. (2006). Question understanding aid (QUAID): A Web facility that helps survey methodologists improve the comprehension of questions. *Public Opinion Quarterly, 70*(1), 1–20.

Groves, R. M. (1989). *Survey errors and survey costs.* New York: John Wiley.

Groves, R. M. (2006). Nonresponse rates and nonresponse bias in household surveys. *Public Opinion Quarterly, 70*(5), 641–675.

Groves, R. M., & Couper, M. P. (1998). *Nonresponse in household interview surveys.* New York: John Wiley.

Groves, R. M., et al. (2006). Experiments in producing nonresponse bias. *Public Opinion Quarterly, 70*(5), 720–736.

Groves, R. M., Dillman, D. A., Eltinge, J. L., & Little, R. J. A. (Eds.). (2002) *Survey nonresponse.* New York: John Wiley.

Groves, R. M., Fowler, F. J., Couper, M. P., Lepkowski, J. M., Singer, E., & Tourangeau, R. (2004). *Survey methodology.* New York: John Wiley.

Groves, R. M., & Kahn, R. L. (1979). *Surveys by telephone.* New York: Academic Press.

Groves, R. M., & Lyberg, L. (1988). An overview of nonresponse issues in telephone surveys. In R. M. Groves, P. N. Biemer, L. E. Lyberg, J. T. Massey, W. L. Nichols II, & J. Waksberg (Eds.), *Telephone survey methodology* (pp. 191–212). New York: John Wiley.

Groves, R.M., Presser, S., & Dipko, S. (2004) The role of topic interest in survey participation decisions. *Public Opinion Quarterly, 68*(1), 2–31.

Hansen, S. E., & Couper, M. P. (2004). Usability testing to evaluate computer-assisted instruments. In S. Presser et al. (Eds.), *Methods for testing and evaluating survey questionnaires* (pp. 337–360). New York: John Wiley.

Harkness, J. A., Van de Vijver, F. J. R., & Mohler, P. P. (2003). *Cross-cultural survey methods.* New York: John Wiley.

Heberlein, T., & Baumgartner, R. (1978). Factors affecting response rates to mailed questionnaires: A quantitative analysis of the published literature. *American Sociological Review, 43,* 447–462.

Henry, G. T. (1990). *Practical sampling.* Newbury Park, CA: Sage.

Henson, R., Roth, A., & Cannell, C. (1977). Personal versus telephone interviews: The effect of telephone reinterviews on reporting of psychiatric symptomatology. In C. Cannell, L. Oksenberg, & J. Converse (Eds.), *Experiments in interviewing techniques: Field experiments in health reporting, 1971–1977* (pp. 205–219). Hyattsville, MD: National Center for Health Services Research.

Hochstim, J. (1967). A critical comparison of three strategies of collecting data from households. *Journal of the American Statistical Association, 62,* 976–989.

Houtkoop-Steenstra, H. (2000). *Interaction and the standardized survey interview: The living questionnaire.* Cambridge, UK: Cambridge University Press.

Hyman, H., Feldman, J., & Stember, C. (1954). *Interviewing in social research.* Chicago: University of Chicago Press.

Jabine, T. B., Straf, M. L., Tanur, J. M., & Tourangeau, R. (Eds.). (1984). *Cognitive aspects of survey methodology: Building a bridge between disciplines.* Washington, DC: National Academy Press.

James, J., & Bolstein, R. (1990). The effect of monetary incentives and follow-up mailings on the response rate and the response quality in mail surveys. *Public Opinion Quarterly, 54*(3), 346–361.

Jobber, D. (1984). Response bias in mail surveys: Further evidence. *Psychological Reports, 54,* 981–984.

Kalton, G. (1983). *Introduction to survey sampling.* Beverly Hills, CA: Sage.

Kaplowitz, M. D., Hadlock, T. D., & Levine, R. (2004). A comparison of Web and mail survey response rates. *Public Opinion Quarterly, 68*(1), 94–101.

Keeter, S., Kennedy, C., Dimock, M., Best, J., & Craighill, P. (2006). Gauging the impact of growing nonresponse on estimates from a national RDD telephone survey. *Public Opinion Quarterly, 70*(5), 759–770.

Keeter, S., Miller, C., Kohut, A., Groves, R. M., & Presser, S. (2000). Consequences of reducing nonresponse in a national telephone survey. *Public Opinion Quarterly, 64*(2), 125–148.

Kish, L. (1949). A procedure for objective respondent selection within the household. *Journal of the American Statistical Association, 44,* 380–387.

Kish, L. (1962). Studies of interviewer variance for attitudinal variables. *Journal of the American Statistical Association, 57,* 92–115.

Kish, L. (1965). *Survey sampling.* New York: John Wiley.

Krosnick, J. A., Judd, C. M., & Wittenbrink, B. (2007). The measurement of attitudes. In D. Albarracin, B. T. Johnson, & M. P. Zanna (Eds.), *The handbook of attitudes* (pp. 21–78). Mahwah, NJ: Lawrence Erlbaum.

Lavrakas, P. J., Stuttles, C. D., Steeh, C., & Fienberg, H. (2007). The state of surveying cell phone numbers in the United States in 2007 and beyond. *Public Opinion Quarterly, 71*(5), 814–854.

Lepkowski, J. M. (1988). Telephone sampling methods in the United States. In R. M. Groves, P. N. Biemer, L. E. Lyberg, J. T. Massey, W. L. Nichols II, & J. Waksberg (Eds.), *Telephone survey methodology* (pp. 73–98). New York: John Wiley.

Lessler, J. T., & Forsyth, B. H. (1996). A coding system for appraising questionnaires. N. A. Schwartz & S. Sudman (Eds.), *Answering questions* (pp. 259–292). San Francisco: Jossey-Bass.

Lessler, J. T., & Kalsbeek, W. D. (1992). *Nonsampling error in surveys.* New York: John Wiley.

Lessler, J., & Tourangeau, R. (1989). Questionnaire design in the cognitive research laboratory. *Vital & Health Statistics,* Series 6, 1. Washington, DC: Government Printing Office.

Likert, R. (1932). A technique for measurement of attitudes. *Archives of Psychology,* 140.

Locander, W., Sudman, S., & Bradburn, N. (1976). An investigation of interview method, threat and response distortion. *Journal of the American Statistical Association, 71,* 269–275.

Lohr, S. L. (1998). *Sampling design and analysis.* New York: Brooks/Cole.

Mangione, T., Hingson, R., & Barret, J. (1982). Collecting sensitive data: A comparison of three survey strategies. *Sociological Methods and Research, 10*(3), 337–346.

Marin, G., & Marin, B. V. (1991). *Research with Hispanic populations.* Newbury Park, CA: Sage.

Marquis, K., Cannell, C., & Laurent, A. (1972). Reporting health events in household interviews: Effects of reinforcement, question length, and reinterviews. *Vital & Health Statistics,* Series 2, 45. Washington, DC: Government Printing Office.

McDowell, I. (2003). *Measuring health: A guide to rating scales and questionnaires* (3rd ed.). Oxford, UK: Oxford University Press.

McHorney, C. A., Kosinsky, M., & Ware, J. E. (1994). Comparisons of the cost and quality of norms for the SF-36 Health Survey by mail versus phone interviews: Results from a national survey. *Medical Care, 32*(6), 551–567.

Miller, P. V., & Cannell, C. F. (1977). Communicating measurement objectives in the interview. In P. Hirsch, P. V. Miller, & F. G. Kline (Eds.), *Strategies for communication research* (pp. 127–152). Beverly Hills: Sage.

National Commission for the Protection of Human Subjects of Biomedical and Behavioral Research. (1979). *Belmont report: Ethical principles and guidelines for the protection of human subjects of research.* Washington, DC: Government Printing Office.

Nichols, W. L., Baker, R. P., & Martin, J. (1997). The effect of new data collection technologies on survey data quality. In L. Lyberg et al. (Eds.), *Survey measurement and process quality* (pp. 221–248). New York: John Wiley.

Office of Management and Budget. (2006). *Standards and guidelines for statistical surveys.* Washington, DC: Author.

Oksenberg, L., Cannell, C., & Kalton, G. (1991). New strategies of pretesting survey questions. *Journal of Official Statistics, 7*(3), 349–366.

Payne, S. (1951). *The art of asking questions.* Princeton, NJ: Princeton University Press.

Penne, M. A., Lessler, J. T., Beiler, G., & Caspar, R. (1998). Effects of experimental and audio computer-assisted self-interviewing (ACASI) on reported drug use in the HSDA. In *Proceedings,* 1998 (section on survey research methods; pp. 744–749). Alexandria, VA: American Statistical Association.

Presser, S., Rothgeb, J. M., Couper, M. P., Lessler, J. T., Martin, E., Martin, J., & Singer, E. (Eds.). (2004). *Methods of testing and evaluating survey questionnaires.* Hoboken, NJ: John Wiley.

Rizzo, L., Brick, J. M., & Park, I. (2004). A minimally intrusive method for sampling persons in random-digit dial surveys. *Public Opinion Quarterly, 68*(2), 267–274.

Robinson, D., & Rhode, S. (1946). Two experiments with an anti-Semitism poll. *Journal of Abnormal Psychology, 41,* 136–144.

Robinson, J. P. (1989). Poll review: Survey organization differences in estimating public participation in the arts. *Public Opinion Quarterly, 53*(3), 397–414.

Robinson, J. P., Shaver, P. R., & Wrightsman, L. S. (Eds.). (1997). *Measures of personality and social psychological attitudes* (Vol. 1). New York: Harcourt Brace.

Saris, W., & Andrews, F. (1991). Evaluation of measurement instrument using a structural modeling approach. In P. Biemer, R. Groves, L. Lyberg, N. A. Mathiowetz, & S. Sudman (Eds.), *Measurment errors in surveys* (pp. 575–597). New York: John Wiley.

Schaeffer, N. C. (1992). Interview: Conversation with a purpose or conversation? In P. Biemer, R. Groves, L. Lyberg, N. A. Mathiowetz, & S. Sudman (Eds.), *Measurment errors in surveys* (pp. 367–393). New York: John Wiley.

Schober, M. F., & Conrad, F. G. (1997). Conversational interviewing. *Public Opinion Quarterly, 61*(4), 576–602.

Schuman, H., & Converse, J. (1971). The effects of black and white interviewers on black responses in 1968. *Public Opinion Quarterly, 35,* 44–68.

Schuman, H., & Presser, S. (1981). *Question and answers in attitude surveys.* New York: Academic Press.

Sieber, J. (1992). *Planning ethically responsible research: Developing an effective protocol.* Newbury Park, CA: Sage.

Singer, E. (2002). The use of incentives to reduce nonresponse in household surveys. In R. M. Groves, D. A. Dillman, J. E. Eltinge, & R. J. A. Little (Eds.), *Survey nonresponse* (pp. 163–177). New York: John Wiley.

Singer, E., Van Hoewyk, J., Gebler, N., Raghunnathan, T., & McGanagle, K. (1999). The effect of incentives on response rates in interviewer-mediated surveys, *Journal of Official Statistics, 15*(2), 217–230.

Singer, E., Van Hoewyk, J., & Maher, M. P. (2000). Experiments with incentives in telephone surveys. *Public Opinion Quarterly, 64*(2), 171–188.

Sirken, M. G., Herrmann, D. J., Schechter, S., Schwarz, N., Tanur, J. M., & Tourangeau, R. (1999). (Eds.). *Cognition and survey research.* New York: John Wiley.

Suchman, L., & Jordan, B. (1990). Interactional troubles in face-to-face survey interviews. *Journal of the American Statistical Association, 85,* 232–241.

Sudman, S. (1967). *Reducing the cost of surveys.* Chicago: Aldine.

Sudman, S. (1976). *Applied sampling.* New York: Academic Press.

Sudman, S., & Bradburn, N. (1982). *Asking questions.* San Francisco: Jossey-Bass.

Tanur, J. M. (1991). *Questions about questions.* New York: Russell Sage.

Tarnai, J., & Moore, D. L. (2004). Methods for testing and evaluating computer-assisted questionnaires. In S. Presser et al. (Eds.), *Methods for testing and evaluating survey questionnaires* (pp. 319–338). New York: John Wiley.

Thurstone, L., & Chave, E. (1929). *The measurement of attitude.* Chicago: University of Chicago Press.

Tourangeau, R., Rips, L., & Rasinski, K. (2000). *The psychology of survey response.* Cambridge, UK: Cambridge University Press.

Tourangeau, R., & Smith, T. W. (1998). Collecting sensitive data with different modes of data collection. In M. P. Couper et al. (Eds.), *Computer assisted survey information collection* (pp. 431–453). New York: John Wiley.

Turner, C. F., et al. (1998). Automated self-interviewing and the survey measurement of sensitive behaviors. In M. P. Couper et al. (Eds.), *Computer assisted survey information collection* (pp. 455–473). New York: John Wiley.

Turner, C. F., & Martin, E. (1984). *Surveying subjective phenomena.* New York: Russell Sage.

Villarroel, M. A., et al. (2006). Same-gender sex in the United States: Impact of T-ACASI on prevalence estimates. *Public Opinion Quarterly, 70*(2), 166–196.

Waksberg, J. (1978). Sampling methods for random-digit dialing. *Journal of the American Statistical Association, 73,* 40–46.

Ware, J. (1987). Standards for validating health measures: Definition and content. *Journal of Chronic Diseases, 40,* 473–480.

Warriner, K., Goyder, J., Jersten, H., Hohner, P., & McSpurren, K. (1996). Cash versus lotteries versus charities in mail surveys. *Public Opinion Quarterly, 60*(4), 542–562.

Weiss, C. (1968). Validity of welfare mothers' interview responses. *Public Opinion Quarterly, 32,* 622–633.

Willis, G. B. (2005). *Cognitive interviewing.* Thousand Oaks, CA: Sage.

Willis, G. B., DeMaio, T., & Harris-Kojetin, B. (1999). Is the bandwagon headed to the methodicalogical promised land? Evaluating the validity of cognitive interviewing techniques. In M. G. Sirken, D. J. Herrmann, S. Schechter, N. Schwarz, J. M. Tanur, & R. Tourangeau (Eds.), *Cognition and survey research* (pp. 133–154). New York: John Wiley.

Wilson, B. F., Alman, B. M., Whitaker, K., & Callegro, M. (2004). How good is good? Comparing numerical ratings of response options for two versions of the self-assessed health status questions. *Journal of Official Statistics, 20*(2), 379–391.

Author Index

Marrett, C., 164
Martin, E., 7, 110, 111, 179
Martin, J., 151
Mathiowetz, N., 53
McDowell, I., 112, 118
McGanagle, K., 58
McHorney, C. A., 74
McNeeley, M. E., 132
McSpurren, K., 59
Meehl, P., 16, 88
Miller, C., 53
Miller, K. J., 151
Miller, P. V., 53, 139
Mohler, P. P., 96
Moore, D. L., 122, 124

Nichols, W. L., 151

Odom, D., 132
Oksenberg, L., 6, 92, 112, 123, 128, 138, 139

Park, I., 36
Payne, S., 5
Penne, M. A., 109
Presser, S., 5, 34, 53, 54, 73, 95, 101, 104, 111, 115, 119

Raghunnathan, T., 58
Rasinski, K., 92, 105
Redline, C. D., 122, 124
Rhode, S., 132
Riesman, D., 133
Rips, L., 92, 105
Rizzo, L., 36
Robinson, D., 132
Robinson, J. P., 66, 112
Roman, A. M., 60, 74
Roth, A., 75
Rothgeb, J. M., 119

Sadowsky, S. A., 124
Saris, W., 16
Schaeffer, N. C., 96, 140
Schechter, S., 107
Schober, N. F., 7, 94, 140, 141
Schuman, H., 73, 95, 101, 104, 111, 132
Schwarz, N., 73, 107
Shaver, P. R., 112
Shuttles, C. D., 34
Sieber, J., 60, 164, 165, 167
Silver, B., 132
Singer, E., 58
Sirken, M. G., 107
Smith, T. W., 74, 109
Stafford, F. P., 107
Starer, A., 34
Steeh, C., 34
Stember, C., 6
Strack, F., 73
Straf, M. L., 107
Stringfellow, V., 52
Suchman, L., 140
Sudman, S., 20, 65, 108, 111, 115, 132
Swinehart, J., 122

Tamai, J., 124
Tanur, J. M., 92, 107, 139
Tarnai, J., 74, 104, 109, 122
Thurstone, L., 5, 100
Tourangeau, R., 74, 92, 105, 107, 119, 109
Tracy, P. E., 109
Tucker, C., 34
Turner, C. F., 7, 74, 109, 110, 111, 179

Vande de Vijver, F. J. R., 96
van der Zouwen, J., 74, 109
Van Hoewyk, J., 58
Villarroel, M. A., 109

Subject Index

About the Author

Floyd J. Fowler, Jr., is a graduate of Wesleyan University and received a Ph.D. from the University of Michigan in 1966. He has been a Senior Research Fellow at the Center for Survey Research at UMass Boston since 1971. He was Director of the Center for 14 years. Dr. Fowler is the author (or coauthor) of four textbooks on survey methods, as well as numerous research papers and monographs. His recent work has focused on studies of question design and evaluation techniques and applying survey methods to studies of medical care.